HUMAN EMOTION AND ARTIFICIAL INTELLIGENCE

R. SOFIA

To my Son S. Ratish

Contents

Foreword

The facial expressions emote to be a medium of communication through non-verbal signals and emerge to be an essential part of human relations. The automatic facial expressions recognition thus becomes imperative for natural human-machine interaction. It finds scope in the field of behavioral science and in the health care sector, among many others.

Although the human beings perceive the facial expressions almost immediately and effortlessly, the reliable automatic facial expression recognition using a machine assuages to be a challenging task. Despite the existence of numerous approaches, still it requires a fresh framework to offer a comprehensive alternative for arriving at error free recognition.

The focus attempts to identify the normal and the traumatic state of a human being in light of the fact that there arise events and circumstances frequently which may eventually force a person to experience a psychological pain. Unless definitive measures evolve, it may be difficult for diagnosing the cause to provide remedial solutions.

The emphasis in this dissertation orients to explore the use of hybrid intelligent techniques for analyzing the images obtained and formulate indices that enable the identification of the state of the person. It underlines the need to quantify the features extracted from the image and allow them to undergo training with a variety of artificial neural networks (ANNs) that include the Feedforward Neural Network(FFNN) and Recurrent neural network(RNN), and Adaptive Fuzzy Inference system(ANFIS).

The first effort alleges to measure the dimensions of the images through known procedures and prepare the data base for training the ANNs. The second endeavor relates to the use of FFNN and RNN and engages both the back propagation (BPN) and the BaysianRegularisation based BPN (BRBPN) for training the network with a view to identify the expression of the person that encompasses happy, sad, anger, neutral , disgust and fear using parametric indices.

The third in line augurs the use of ANFIS and introduces the methodology of ANOVA for reducing the number of inputs. However the approach offers to identify the expressions with reliable accuracy. The fourth effort again operates using both FFNN and RNN with the benefits of the ANOVA scheme for identifying the expressions.

The fifth endeavor lays down a procedure for identifying the state of trauma with the help of a target fixed during training for each expression. It creates a threshold to behold the range beyond which it identifies the person to be in a state of trauma. The process involves the use of FFNN and RNN and operates with both the BPN and the BRBPN to facilitate the identification strategy.

The sixth effort benign with ANFIS and ANOVA initially to identify the traumatic state on the same target and threshold based principles. It extends the same to operate the FFNN and RNN with both the BPN and the BRBPN and enables the process of identification from the target and threshold mechanisms.

The entire study works on networks with forty and twenty four input layers respectively, twenty hidden layers and one output layer and operates with the Hyperbolic tan sigmoid activation function in thehidden layer and linear activation function at the output layer on a MATLAB portal to execute the identification philosophy. It extracts the results for two definite number of epochs one in the lower and the other in the upper end in order to establish the applicability of the algorithm.

The results in terms of parametric indices open up interesting claims and seek a huge space for its use in far reaching applications in the real world. The robustness of the indices serves to establish a sense of reliability in the identification process and invites to open fresh dimensions for the role of intelligent techniques.

Preface

Although the human beings perceive the facial expressions almost immediately and effortlessly, the reliable automatic facial expression recognition using a machine assuages to be a challenging task. Despite the existence of numerous approaches, still it requires a fresh framework to offer a comprehensive alternative for arriving at error free recognition.

The focus attempts to identify the normal and the traumatic state of a human being in light of the fact that there arise events and circumstances frequently which may eventually force a person to experience a psychological pain. Unless definitive measures evolve, it may be difficult for diagnosing the cause to provide remedial solutions.

Acknowledgements

I thank my Husband and My son..

Prologue

CHAPTER 6 TRAUMA IDENTIFICATION USING FFNN AND BRRNN

Methodology

Scope for future work
REFERENCES

● xxi ●

ONE
INTRODUCTION

GENERAL

The interaction of human beings with computers appears to be exciting and becoming a necessity of the present environment, consequent to which in the recent years many branches of the technology continue to explore the ability of facial and emotion recognition.

The scope envisages expanding the horizons in light of the need to arbitrate with the sensitivities of the person and arrive at identifying the state of the mind. Since 1970 when Paul Ekman started his research on facial expressions and found that the facial expression of emotion fosters to be biological in origin and not determined by culture, a lot of progress evinces on emotion recognition.

The facial expression analysis deals with analysis of different facial motion changes by extraction of facial parameters. A typical system extracts number of facial parameters from an image, and classifies the image into the set of defined expressions. There exist six universally recognized expressions viz, Angry, Disgust, Fear, Happy, Sad and Neutral.

The exercise originates with a requisite to process the image in the sense it involves a procedure to perform certain operations and acquire useful information from it. It relates to a type of signal processing in which the input represents an image and the output may be characteristics/features associated with that image. The processed image augurs to extract features in the form of eyes, eyebrows and mouth to standout to find the facial expression.

According to Hyisung C. Hwang and David Matsumoto (2016) the human emotion can be delineated in two major ways that be-hive either an indirect or direct approach. The indirect method involves the observer judgments of the facial expressions and the direct category which requires a measurement of the facial muscle movements. The process echoes to classify the facial configurations as emotional expressions based on a taxonomy or dictionary of sorts.

The direct procedure in recent times engages the role of local binary pattern (LBP),principle component analysis (PCA), action unit (AU), active shape model (ASM), Gabor filter and region of interest (ROI) localization methodfor identifying the human emotion.

The process of finding out the facial expression in Allaerts et al., (2017) relies on matching with the Morphable Model, in the sense it determines the pose, shape and expression and impinges to fit with the Morphable model and there from identify the human emotion. It records that anger and surprise become less impacted by the face registration and the system experiences difficulty in differentiating between the disgust, fear with anger and surprise.

A descriptor in Daniel et al., (2017)creates a set based on areas and angles of triangles formed by the landmarks from face images. The descriptors serve to classify the facial expressions with the conditional random field and the citation KNN classifier.

The LBP feature extraction technique in Sunil et al., (2016)uses only the informative region of face and classifies the human emotion using the SVM Classifier. It assumes the neutral expression as the base and calculates from the neutral facial features as to how much the facial features of the other expression differs.

The Gabor filter based feature extraction in Dagar et al., (2016) allows the classification using NN and extracts the facial attributes using PCA. The region detection algorithm in Dhrubajoti et al., (2015) extracts the mouth, eyebrows and eyes from the selected face regions and classifies the expression with hidden markovmodel(HMM).

The primary goal owes to formulate a novel facial expression recognition and trauma identification system using various soft computing techniques. It necessitates system level design, where in it engages the building blocks to design the system. A facial expression recognition system usually consists of multiple components, each of which becomes responsible for one task.

The equally important stage orients to the algorithm level design where the focus centers on the classifier, which forms the core of a recognition system, trying to use the algorithms that attempt improve the performance.

The intelligent techniques particularly the neural networks (NN) invite considerable attention in the pursuit of being a classifier and serve as a precursor tool of being able to identify the emotions of a person. The FFNN (FeedForward Neural Network), the RNN (Recurrent Neural Network), the ANFIS (Adaptive Neuro Fuzzy Inference System) find an increasing use among the varieties of the networks in vogue.

The choice of the algorithm for operating the network echoes an equally important space in order that it ensures the success of the task on hand. The emphasis in the present perspective revolves around the use of Backpropagation and the ANOVA for identifying the normal and the trauma states.

1.4 OBJECTIVE OF THE RESEARCH WORK

The main aim of the dissertation assuages to evolve neural network based mechanisms for

- Recognizingthe various facial expressionsthat include HAPPY, ANGER, SAD, NEUTRAL, DISGUST and FEAR of a person.
- Identifying the traumatic state of a person with an ability to distinguish from the normal being with a choice of six targets and precise thresholds.

The endeavor envisages the use of a MATLAB based simulation platform for evaluating the performance of the network through parametric indices.

1.8 ORGANIZATION OF THE THESIS

The first chapter introduces the fundamental preludes, frames the objectives and lays down the organization of the thesis.

The second chapter provides the overview of various studies used in the field of facial features recognition

The third chapter underscores the issues relating to the measuring the dimensions of the features.

The fourth chapter explains the recognition of the emotions of a person using FFNN and RNN.

The fifth chapter brings in the use of ANFIS along with the concept of ANOVA for recognizing the emotion and attempts to implement ANOVA for FFNN and RNN.

The sixth chapter orients to identify the traumatic using FFNN and RNN

The seventh chapter engages the principles of ANOVA on ANFIS and FFNN and RNN for identifying the state of trauma.

The eighth chapter concludes the dissertation with a summary of the contributions, limitation of the methodology and lays down the directions for future scope.

TWO
LITERATURE REVIEW

CHAPTER 2
LITERATURE REVIEW

2.1 General

The goal of this thesis was to design and implement a functional framework for the classification of facial expressions present on the faces of individuals in images. The link between the emotion felt by an individual and the facial expression they display is both reflexive and reflective. However, expressions are generally accepted to be the primary observable response. Thus, for computer vision purposes, the shortest route to investigating human emotion cuts directly through the field of facial expression research. Naturally, human emotions are an area of great interest for many practical applications, rendering facial expressions research a popular topic.

2.2 Historical Review

Emotions recognition can be done through different modalities, such as speech, facial expression, body gestures etc. Emotion recognition through facial expression has attracted a lot of interest in last few decades. Expression of our face says a lot without speaking. A facial expression is one or more position of muscles beneath the skin of the face. According to one set of controversial theories, these movements convey the emotional state of an individual to observers. Facial expression is form of non verbal communication. They are primary of conveying social message between humans

Darwin in the year 1872 was the first to suggest the correlation between the facial expression and emotion. Based on his observations, demonstrated the universality of facial expression by defining the three principles. He proposed that, these principles account for most of the expressions and gestures used by man.

1. The principle of serviceable associated habits: it emphasizes the importance of habits in formulating certain expressions in man.

2. The principle of antithesis: this principle gives the explanation of certain expressions which are not formulated by habits but are shown when an exact opposite state of mind to the habits is induced.

3. The principle of actions due to the constitution of the nervous system, independently from the will, and independently to a certain extent of Habit: this principle gives an account of those expressions that are a direct result of the action of nervous system and are independent of will or habits.

In the year 1972 Ekman, Friesen and Ellsworth works on the idea of Darwin and found that according to psychology perspective facial expression were culture specific like any culture had its own verbal language; emotion had its own language of facial expression. Mc carter and Tokmins in the year 1964 gives the first study demonstrating that facial expressions were reliable associate with certain emotional state. In the psychological research one can express his feelings and attitude by speaking i.e., by saying up to 7% through his vocal expressions upto 98% and 55% through his facial expressions as stated by A.Meharabian(1968). This shows that facial expression plays an important role for an individual too express their intention attitude, feelings and emotional state and other non-verbal messages in speech communication. Facial expression shows the mood or emotional state of an individual how he is feeling at a particular moment like sad, happy, anger.

2.3 Emotion Detection through Facial Expression

According to Hyisung C. Hwang and David Matsumoto (2016) human emotion can be delineated into two major ways they are

1. _Indirect Method_

Indirect approaches involve observer judgments of produced facial expressions: the emotions of the expressors are inferred through the obtained judgments

2. Direct Method

Direct approaches involve direct measurement of the facial muscle movements that are produced: researchers using direct approaches than classify the observed facial configurations as emotional expressions (or other types of classifications) based on a taxonomy or dictionary of sorts.

Fig 2.1: Techniques used in direct method extracting facial features which in turn help in identifying the facial expression through which emotion of the human being can be identified. (Shows the existing method with their disadvantages)

As shown in above figure 2.1, emotion of the human can be measured using two methods they are: **Indirect Method** it is based on observer judgments and communication approaches, **Direct Method** used in recent days for identifying human emotion are LBP(Local Binary Pattern), PCA(Principle component Analysis), AU(Action Unit), ASM(Active Shape Model), Gabor filter, ROI(Region of Interest) localization method and their disadvantage as shown in the figure above.

In Allaerts et al., (2017)finding out the facial expression based on matching with the Morphable Model, ie., finding out the pose, shape and expression and making that fit with the Morphable model and finding out the human emotion, and they say that Anger, surprise are less impacted by face registration and system gets difficulty in differentiating between the disgust, fear with anger, surprise. Daniel et al., (2017)A descriptor is set based on areas and angles of triangles formed by the landmarks from face images. And then these descriptor are used for facial expression classification with conditional Random field and citation KNN classifier. Sunil et al., (2016) uses LBP feature extraction technique (uses only the informative region of face) and classify the human emotion using the SVM Classifier. Here the neutral expression is taken as base and from the neutral facial features how much the facial features of other expression differ is calculated.Dagar et al., (2016)Gabor filter based feature extraction and classified using Neural Network and the facial attributes are extracted using PCA. Yeshudas et al., (2015)LBP is used for Facial Feature extraction and the neural network is used as the classifier.Dhrubajoti et al., (2015)Selected face regions such as mouth, eyebrows and eyes are extracted by using region detection algorithm and classify the expression with Hidden Markov Model(HMM). Anas et al., (2016)Uses various feature extraction techniques such as ACM(Active

Contour Model), ASM(Active Shape Model), AAM(Active Appearance Model), CLM(Constrained Local Model) and compares its advantages and disadvantages. Dileep et al., (2016)Human Emotion has been classified with the help of eyes and mouth using susan edges. Satyananda et al., (2016) Uses Gabor filter for identifying emotion. Tuhin et al., (2017)Appearance based model of eyes and mouth for identifying emotion. Latifa et al., (2017)Euclidean and Mahattan distance measure for facial expression classification. Pawel et al., (2017)Full face is considered and based on the Action Unit the emotions are identified.(Twishaet al.,(2017), Khoodijah et al.,(2016), Nazima et al., (2016), Neha et al., (2016), Samiksha et al.,(2015), Shubhada et al., (2015), Nidhi et al., (2017), Shinde et al., (2014), Archana et al., (2016)) are survey paper about various techniques of extracting features and emotion identification using various classifier.Hyisung(2016), Annett et al.,(2017), Paul et al., (2015) gives the very good detail research work for the human emotion identification.

2.4Procedural steps involved in facial expression Recognition

The major procedural steps involved in facial expression recognition namely face detection, feature extraction and classification. Dimensionality reduction can also be included based on the computational complexity and feature vector length. Different systems for perceiving human facial expressions from face pictures have been proposed and their execution has been assessed with databases of face pictures with varieties in expressions. The generalized procedure followed for facial expression recognition is shown as a block diagram in figure 2.1. The images which are to be classified form the test image set and in order to train the system some predefined cues are to be given as input. This is implemented in the form of features extracted from the set of training images. The training set is a combination of images from different classes and distinguishable features are extracted for common classes to provide information cues to the classifier.

Fig. 2.2 Generalized procedure of Facial expression recognition

2.4.1 Face Detection

Face detection has two main approaches

- Skin color based segmentation: in which area and color of the sin are major parameters for classifying face from non face. The images are represented in YCbCr(Y is the luma component, CB and CR are the blue difference and red difference chroma components), RGB(Red-Green-Blue Component of the color) and HCI(Hue-Chroma-Luminance) color models and a new model is proposed by combining them. As skin color becomes an important cue for the presence of face in an image. R. Singh et al.,(2003) have proposed detection of face using skin color. This procedure becomes inefficient with movement and varying illumination and also when background is of the similar color skin much false detection are present. Another hindrance of skin color is it is non uniform for all races and varies with ageing.
- Boosted cascade of simple features:P. Viola and M. J. Jones(2004) proposedviola Jones algorithm in which Haar like features are cascaded in each stage and face class is filtered out from non face classes using Adaboost algorithm.

2.4.2 Preprocessing

Preprocessing of facial images is an essential step to enhance and condition facial expression recognition. Obtaining a pure facial expression image with normalized intensity accompanied by uniformity in shape and size as mention by X. Tan and B. Triggs (2010) is the prime motive of preprocessing. It also eliminates the effect of uneven illumination and improper lighting conditions. The preprocessing procedure adopted here as a part of this system performs the following two steps in converting an image to a normalized pure expression image for feature extraction.

- Image is taken from the JAFFE database is cropped by removing the background and having only the face part
- That face part undergo a contrast adjustment and gamma correction has been done to the value of 1.25, where the Gamma value greater than 1, expands the lighter regions and compresses the darker regions of the original image.

2.4.3 Facial Feature Location

The information about facial expressions is contained in various regions of the face. Depending on the feature extraction method used, regions of the face are located and further features are extracted. Facial feature extraction from regions of interest improves recognition results significantly. Facial feature location takes place prior to feature extraction: it preselects certain regions of the face and leaves out uninteresting regions.

Permanent facial Features

Relevant face regions are regions containing permanent facial features which form the facial expressions. These are normally the eyes, nose, eyebrows and the mouth but can also be permanent facial furrows which come with age. The deformation of those gives important information about the expression. Systems which track facial features in moving pictures rely on *such permanent features.*

Transient Facial Features

In addition to permanent facial features that move and change their shape, facial movement also causes facial wrinkles, known as transient facial features. Transient facial features such as wrinkles that appear around the eyes, forehead and mouth occur often in combination with facial expression displayed with high intensities. They are crucial for detection of certain AUs (Action Units).

Whole face

A face, separated from its background, can be used completely for feature extraction with no previous facial feature detection involved. It is useful to recognize facial expressions holistically. Holistic descriptions of the face preserve all the information in the face: they preserve regions which would be lost using only regions obtained from positions of detected facial features.

2.4.4 Feature extraction:

The following four approaches, shown in figure 2.5, are widely used for detecting human face features: geometric based, appearance based, template based, and color based.

- *Geometry based approach:* for face or face parts detection works on geometric relationship between invariant features using statistical models. Geometry based techniques includes distance between two eyes, distance between nose and lips etc. Under geometry based technique, edge detection techniques are also used for detecting face parts. Geometric feature based have advantages like independent from scaling, rotation independency, and efficient in execution time as compared to other methods. Viola Jones algorithm gives good results with efficient computation time for face and face parts detection. As geometry based approach is one of the important method for the feature extraction.
- *Appearance based approach:* to learn "template" characteristic it makes use of statistical analysis and machine learning technique. Neural network, support vector machine and Principal Component analysis(PCA) are widely used techniques of appearance based approach by it is relatively complex to implement. Its high dimensionality requires many training samples to train data. Bartlett and her colleagues extend the system by using fully automatic face and eye detection. For facial expression analysis, they employ Gabor wavelets as appearance features. Majumder et al., (2014), proposed their work of identifying facial expression using Appearance based Approach.
- *Template matching approach:* finds correlation values with a standard face pattern for face contour, eyes, nose, and mouth. Template matching method defines its own templates such as geometric templates. This approach is simple to implement. However,drawbacks of these methods are that these methods cannot deal with variation in

scale, pose and shape which was dealt by Aann Zane et al., in (2014)

**Fig. 2.3: General Approaches for feature
extraction
of human face**

- _Color based approach:_Xiaoning Chen et al.,(2015) proposed a work of identifying facial expression detection using color based approach where the Color models such as RGB color model andYCbCr color model for face parts detection. This approach uses skin color information for segmentation of face. But this approach can also detect non-face skin color portion. For finding non-skin region form face, color based approach could be used.

2.4.5 Classification

The last step of AFEA(Automatic Facial Expression Analysis) systems is to recognize facial expression based on the extracted features. Many classifiers have been applied to expression recognition such as neural network (NN), support vector machines (SVM), linear discriminant analysis (LDA), K-nearest neighbor(K-NN), multinomial logistic ridge regression (MLR), hidden Markov models (HMM), tree augmented naive Bayes, RankBoost, and others.

Efficient approaches for classification are mentioned below:

- _Naïve Baycsian(NB) Classifier:_ This is a Probabilistic method that has been shown very effective in many classification problems. This method considers that the presence of a particular feature of a class is unrelated to the presence of any other feature
- Radial Basis Function(RBF): RBF has been used in many applications lie prediction, function approximation and classification. It is more robust and efficient than any other conventional neural network. The RBF has fast learning speed due to the locally tuned neurons. RBF also consider as an approximate neural network by S.M.Lajevardi and Z.M. Hussain (2009).

- _Multilayer Perceptron(MLP):_ MLP is a feed forward neural network that maps sets of input data onto a set of appropriate output. MLP follows supervised learning technique. This supervised learning method also called back propagation for training the network. MLP is an improvisation of the standard linear perceptron and can distinguish data that are not linearly separable which is given by Wikipedia. HayetBoughrara(2014)in his study of facial expression recognition based on a MLP neural using constructive training algorithm works with MLP of three layer. The number of input neurons is equal to the size of related feature vector. Same as, the number of output neurons has 1 for the correct input pattern and 0 for all others output neurons. The hidden layer is constructed using the proposed constructive training algorithm. There are two steps on the realization of the facial expression recognition system using the MLP architecture: the training step and the testing step. The learning algorithm used this study is the standard back-propagation. MLP requires the network architecture definition before the training. This is known that there is no general answer to the problem of defining neural network architecture for the given problem but MLP works wee if the network architecture is properly chosen. MLP neural network is by a trial and error procedure. An alternative is to use constructive algorithms which try to solve the problem by building the architecture of the neural network during its training.

- *Support Vector Machine (SVM):* P. Michel and R. El Kaliouby (2003) It is administered learning models with related learning calculations that dissect information and perceive examples, utilized for classification. It is a binary classifier but can be extended to multiclass classification. SVM is a non-probabilistic binary classification method where classes are separated by boundary and patterns are shown as points in space. SVM being supervised learning method it is reliable tool for classification.
- *Distance classifiers:* like nearest classifier and KNN classifier which give the minimum distance class as detected class of test image efficiency of distance classifiers is les but their hardware implementation easy.
- *Artificial neural networks:* are efficient methods to classify samples with large number of attributes. They take help of a back propagation algorithm such that every layer is trained efficiently with numerous iterations minimizing classification error in adhering to the correct class.

2.5 Facial Expression Database

Work continues in developing good databases(Nazima et al., 2016) for facial expression containing emotional content. A wiki had been created to aid researchers in locating emotional expression databases: Many of these databases consist of static facial expressions (images) with little work devoted to video sequences. As the debate continues among which type of system works best, and they found the following databases to be referenced more than any others in studies of expression recognition.

1. JAFFE Database
2. Cohan-Kanade Database

From this we have taken **JAFFE Database** for our research work for identifying emotion of the person through facial expression with the help of facial features.

2.6 Matlab for Image Processing

- A very large (and growing) database of built-in algorithms for image processing and computer vision applications
- MATLAB allows you to test algorithms immediately without recompilation. You can type something at the command line or execute a section in the editor and immediately see the results, greatly facilitating algorithm development.
- The MATLAB Desktop environment, which allows you to work interactively with your data, helps you to keep track of files and variables, and simplifies common programming/debugging tasks
- The ability to read in a wide variety of both common and domain-specific image formats.
- Clearly written documentation with many examples, as well as online resources such as web seminars ("webinars").
- Bi-annual updates with new algorithms, features, and performance enhancements
- If you are already using MATLAB for other purposes, such as simulation, optimization, statistics, or data analysis, then there is a very quick learning curve for using it in image processing.
- The ability to process both still images and video.
- Technical support from a well-staffed, professional organization (assuming your maintenance is up-to-date)
- A large user community with lots of free code and knowledge sharing
- The ability to auto-generate C code, using MATLAB Coder, for a large (and growing) subset of image processing and mathematical functions, which you could then use in other environments, such as embedded systems or as a component in other software.
- Matlab Doesn't require compiler to execute like C,C++. It just executes each sentence as it is written in code. This increase productivity and coding efficiency. It is higher level language. Using Matlab Coder the codes written in Matlab can be converted to C++, Java, Python, .Net etc. This makes this language more versatile. So, scientific

theories can be implemented in other languages also. And those library files can be directly implemented in other languages.

- Matlab has inbuilt rich library of Neural Network, Fuzzy Logic, Simulink, Power System, Hydraulics, Electrical, Communication, Electromagnetism, etc. Thus developing any scientific simulation is easy to do using such rich library.Disadvantage is its cost of License. It's very costly user has to buy each and every module and pay for it. Disadvantage is during cross compiling or converting Matlab to other language code is very difficult. It's very difficult or requires deep Matlab knowledge to deal with all errors. Matlab is not suggested to make any product. Because, Matlab doesn't create application deployment(installation) like task (like setup files and other executable which copies during installation).

2.7 Overview of existing approach

In the method proposed by S.Kherchaoui et al (2014)., as a first step they detect the face and facial features to extract the face centered region and as the next step they go for the normalization of this interest region and edge extraction. At this step they found the facial edges which they use for calculating the Euclidean distance of all pixels that constitute edges and uses Support Vector Machine classifier(SVM) to predict the facial emotion and they make use of JAFFE database. Yi et al., (2010) proposes the system which combines LBP and Gabor features, for facial expression detection.

Premanand et al., (2016) have used Local Directional Number Pattern(LDNP) for extracting features and for classification they use both SVM and FFNN and found that SVM performance is destitute and the FFNN for the proposed method shows the increase in accuracy.Debasmita et al., (2013) uses Eigenspaces(which is a modified method of Eigenfaces approach) which directly classifies a test image as belonging to one of the standard six expressions- anger, disgust, fear, happy, sad or surprise.

Chih et al., have introduced two stage feature extraction at the first stage they use Threshold LBP and in the second stage they extract the most discriminate features from the block-based center-symmetric LBP and finally they use SVM for classification.Varanya et al., (2017) use CK+ database and extract the features using LBP and the extracted features are given to the SVM and ANN for classification and found ANN works better than the SVM.

In the work proposed by Kiran Talele et al., (2016), they use facial expression recognition using efficient local binary pattern(LBP) for feature extraction and artificial neural network(ANN) for classification is presented. Facial feature vectors are obtained using efficient LBP algorithm by considering the blocks of four varied sizes of image dataset. The major focus of this work includes the comparison and analysis of partitioning the blocks of the image to further improve the recognition efficiency, and they found among the various block sizes 64x64 pixels is better.

Prashant et al., (2016) have done a work that do a comparison between the methodologies used for human emotion recognition for face images based on textural analysis and KNN classifier. And this comparative study of facial expression recognition involves Curvelet transform ased Robust LBP, and Distinct LBP features and features derived from DLBP and Gray-Level Co- occurance Matrix (GLCM). And they found that the DLBP and RLBP based feature extraction with KNN classifier gives much better accuracy with lesser algorithmic complexity.

Gengtaozhou et.,(2006) used selective feature extraction method where expressions are roughly classified into three kinds according to the deformation of mouth as 1. Sad, anger, disgust 2. Happy, fear, 3. Surprise and again some if then rules are used to sub classify individual group expressions. Jun Ou et al., (2010) used 28 facial features points and Gabor wavelet filter for facial feature lacalization, PCA for feature extraction and KNN for expression classification.

Uddin, J.J, LEE and T.S. Kim (2009), used Enhanced Independent Component Analysis (EICA) to extract locally independent component features which are further classified by fisher linear Discriminant Analysis(FLDA). Then discrete HMM is used to model different facial expressions. Feature extraction results of various conventional method(PCA, PCA-FLDA, ICA and ECIA) in conjunction with same HMM scheme were compared and comparative analysis is presented in terms of recognition rate. PCA is unsupervised learning method used to extract useful features and 2nd order statistical methodfor deriving orthogonal bases containing the maximum variability and is also used for dimensionality reduction. V. Gomathiet al.,(2010) used uniform local binary pattern(LBP) histogram technique for feature extraction and MANIFS(Multiple Adaptive Neuro fuzzy inference System) for expression recognition.

Murthy et al., (2009) proposed modified PCA (Eigen spaces) for face reconstruction method for expression recognition. They have divided the training set of Cohn Kanade and JAFFE databases into 6 different partitions and Eigen space is constructed for each class, then image sis reconstructed. Mean square error is used as similarity measure for comparing origin and reconstructed image.

HadiSeyedarabi et al., (2004) developed facial expression recognition system for recognizing basic expressions. They have used cross correlation based optical flow method for extracting facial feature vectors. RBF neural network and fuzzy inference system for recognizing basic expressions. Zhengyou Zhang et al., (2006), presented a features extracted from face images for recognizing facial expression. Geometric positions of set of fiducial point and multiscale and multi orientation Gobarwavelet coefficient extracted from the face image at the fiducial points are the two approaches used for feature extraction. These are given to neural network classifier separately of jointly and results were compared.

Comparison of the recognition performance with different types of features shows that Gabor wavelet Coefficient are more powerful than geometric positions.Junhua Li and Li Peng (2008) used feature difference matrix for feature extraction and QNN(Quantum Neural Network) for expression recognition. From the survey, it is observed that various approaches have been used to detect facial features and classified as holistic and feature based methods to extract facial feature from images or video sequences of faces. These are geometry based, appearance based, template based and skin color segmentation based approaches.

The work proposed by Khandait et al., (2011) approach to the problem of automatic facial feature extraction form a still frontal posed image and classification and recognition of facial expression and hence emotion and mood of a person is presented. Feed Forward back propagation neural network is used as a classifier for classifying the expressions of supplied face into seven basic categories like surprise, neutral, sad, disgust, fear, happy and angry, for face portions segmentation and localization, morphological image processing operations are used. Permanent facial features like eyebrows, eyes, mouth and nose are extracted using susan edge detection operator, facial geometry, edge projection analysis.

Michel et al., (2016) works with the four stages the first two stages of the system deal with detecting and cropping the face using image processing, in particular viola-Jones object detection framework. The third stage deals with converting the colors of the cropped image form RGB into gray scale and applying the appropriate smoothing filter. The fourth stage consists of feature extraction using ANN, so as the extracted features are compared with training samples. The final stage classifies the compared with training samples. The final stage classifies given outputs and shows facial expression recognitions results. It then determines whether the subject is happy, angry or in neutral state.

Tai and Chung (2007) when a face image is input, two inner canthi are detected as the reference points for searching the expression features extracted from the contour and displacement of eyebrows, eyes and mouth. Our feature extraction method can reduce the partial influence of shadows and noises. Finally, the expression features are used as the input to an Elman Neural Network of classifiers.

Kunika and Ajay (2017) uses the Viola Jones method for face detection and the facial features are extracted using Gabor filter and the ANN is used for classification and this work uses JAFFE database which show the robustness and better recognition rates for this work. Neha and Navneet (2013) proposed an accurate and high speed emotion detection system. The color and feature-based detections were adopted to find skin-color fast and selected candidate blocks carefully. They used lighting compensation to improve the performance of color-based scheme, and reduce the computation of feature-based scheme. The major contribution of their work is to detect edges of the images and from that edges distance between various features is calculated by using Euclidean distance Formulae. This distance is different for every image posing different emotions. On the basis of this distance emotions are classified.

For efficient detection of spatial expression, many algorithms have been proposed. Ghimireet. al., (2016)proposed extraction of local region specific features and support vector machines for classification of the facial expression. Classification accuracy of 97% was achieved.Shag et. al (2009) applied support vector machine classifiers on the boosted local binary pattern features obtained from different image data sets. The accuracy obtained for jaffe image data set was 81%. Cohn-Kanade database of video signal is classified by Siddiqi et. al using Hidden Conditional Random Fields and a classification accuracy of 93% is achieved. Happy and Routray (2015) implemented facial expression recognition from Jaffe and CK images by determining facial patches. Zhong et.al (2015) also determined facial patches and used them for multitask sparse learning) framework. But facial patches vary for different sets of faces.

Nisha et al(2015), investigation proposed an overview of face detection and expression recognition using artificial neural network with aim to provide recent holistic and feature based approaches. NazilPerveen et al (2012), proposed the fastest neural network technique to classify the expressions is used which classify the face in 0:02:11 seconds. The effective back-propagation network with 6 input neurons, 100 hidden neurons and 7 output neurons is used to train the network. Mehdi AkhariOskuyee 2012, in this paper they use eyes and lip as biometric elements for face emotion recognition. To increase accuracy in face emotion recognition they recommend use of feed forward neural network.

Smriti Tikoo et al , proposed the histogram equivalent of binary and gray images have been computed as the data to check for the recognition. Training of each sample is performed up to 3-4 times to minimize the error and changing the number of neurons in the hidden layer accordingly to obtain a better result. Facial image without dividing into parts have also been applied in the network .

Deepthi.S et al (2013), proposed expression recognition is done using neural networks. Neural networks tend to be black box, they will train and achieve a level of performance but we cannot easily determine how they are making the decision. Dr. Sanjay Kumar et algives the introduction of the face recognition and facial expression recognition and an investigation on the recent previous researches for extracting the effective and efficient method for facial expression recognition.

Jawad Nagi et al(2008), presented a novel face recognition technique that uses features derived from DCT coefficients, along with a SOM-based classifier. Kotsia and Pitas (2007) used geometric deformation features and support vector machines for facial expression detection of Cohn-Kanade database and obtained a classification accuracy of 99.7%. Huang and Tai (2012) used key point descriptors for determining the features and classified the expression using weighted majority voting classifier. The accuracy obtained for jaffe image data set was 93.33%.

Sang-Kwon Sim et al(2016), to recognize expression, the two features were entered in the artificial neural network classifier and these were recognized through error backpropagation learning algorithm. The learning data is a front face image used in JAFFE database: three expressions of expressionless (neutral), happiness, and anger were classified. Shamla Mantri, Kalpana Bapat (2011),showedthe efficiency of achieving the face regonition by neural network using the Matlab.

Manisha et al (2015), used a still image facial expression recognition technique. The facial expression recognition system is found to be 76% accurate.Belal Ahmad et al (2016), usesThe neural network approach based on face recognition, feature extraction and categorization and training is provided to the software to analyze or recognize the emotion. The facial expression recognition system is found to be 92.498333% accurate. Sonali V.Hedaoo et al (2014), use Dynamic Bayesian Network(DBN) for simultaneous facial feature tracking and facial expression recognition. Smriti Tikoo et al (2016), in this paper the facial detection has been carried out using Viola Jones algorithm and recognition of face has been done using Back Propagation Neural Network (BPNN).

Chi et.al (2015) suggested a cloud model of images for expression recognition. The effectiveness of the suggested method is not mentioned. Sarode and Bhatia (2010) extracted intransient facial features and detected four facial expressions. An average accuracy of 81.5% is obtained for four classes of jaffe image data set. Shruti Bansal and Pravin Nagar (2015) used Bezier curves for determining emotions. The accuracy obtained was 70%.

Anagha S. Dhavalikar et al., (2014) involve two process for Automatic facial expression detection by involving simple Euclidean distance method between the feature points and based on this they have achieved 90%-95% recognition rate by using the features such as eyes, nose, mouth using Active Appearance Model(AAM), and the second process is made with ANFIS.

S.P. Kahandit et al.,(2012) features such as eyes, eyebrows mouth and nose are extracted by using SUSAN edge detection operator and face geometry by using JAFFE database and the AFED is done using approaches of ANFIS and

NN with 30 test samples and has achieved recognition rate upto 97.142% and 94.7%. Swathi Mishra et al.,(2015)in this viola Jones face detection technique has been used for face detection and after this features like eyes and mouth are extracted and this is given to ANFIS for Emotion Detection(ED) with KDEF database with 150 images. Swathi Mishra, Avinash Dhole et al., (2016) but ED is done with the Indian image which is database created and it has achieved the recognition rate upto 85.45% with trained images and 38.89% for untrained images with ANFIS

V Gomathi et al.,(2010)here the facial image is segmented into 3 regions form which the uniform local binary pattern texture features distributions are extracted and represented as a histogram descriptor and the ED is recognized using MANFIS. S.P. Khandait et al.,(2013)this paper uses facial geometry algorithm propagation neural network (BPNN) and (ANFIS) for ED by using the JAFFE database and achieve the recognition rate upto 95.33%to 93.33% using BPNN and 95.71% to 95.33% with ANFIS Approach. NicegeorgeBizdoc et al., (2015)here they have used viola jones algorithm for face detection and for tracking in videos they used camshift algorithm. The detected human face is given to Sugeno type decisional fuzzy system, which is based on the variable fuzzy measurements of the face, eyes, eyelid and mouth.

S.P. Khandaitet al.,(2012) curvelet transform is applied on the database images and the curvelet features are obtained and it is compressed using singular value decomposition(SVD). And it is given to classifier such as BPNN and ANFIS for ED. N.M. Jothi swaroopan et al.,(2017)here the feature are extracted using PCA technique which calculate the principal component and it is given for ANFIS for AFED. M.A. Shaha et al.,(2016) this paper achieves high AFED rate than the state of art technique by using ANFIS and the Bezier crves with the helpofJAFEE database and cohnkanade database. ShubhangiGiripunjje, Narendra Bawane et al.,(2007)they have done with speech based emotion classification method by using ANFIS with the help Voice pitch, formants, energy and speaking rate as the babes features.

Derya Yilmaz et al., (2013)they have done a SRS(Snore related sounds) for detection of sleep apnea/hyperpnoea syndrome(SAHS) which prove SVM is better than ANFIS. Ganeshan.R et al., (2014) gives brief review about ANFIS. PijushKanti Ghosh et al., (2014) In this AFED is done by using ANFIS and they have shown that PCA with SVD(Singular Value Decomposition) is superior to PCA in terms AFED rate for Basic emotions. Sasipraba et al., (2015)here the age of a person is estimated with the help of ANFIS. MythiAsaithambi et al., (2012) here the AFED has been done with the help of eyes, lips by using ANFIS as a classifier for detection four basic expressions angry, happy, sad and surprise. Shinde A.R et al.,(2014) a comparative study of facial feature extraction, expression and emotion recognition using ANFIS has been done and concluded that ANFIS can achieve AFED than BPNN. Urvashi N. Agrawal(2013)here the brief review about the ANFIS classifier for emotion recognition has been done.

Recently large amount of contributions were proposed in recognizing expression using dynamic textures features using LBP, Gabor wavelet approach, PCA and Appearance features which in turn increases complexity where their disadvantages are mentioned fig. 2.2. Moreover one cannot show features located with the help of bounding box. Hence, the proposed facial expression recognition system aimed to use image preprocessing and geometry based techniques for feature extraction and given to the FFNN, RNN, ANFIS for expression recognition for the frontal view face images.

1.4OBJECTIVE AND SCOPE OF PRESENT WORK

The primary goal of this research is to design, implement and evaluate a novel facial expression recognition system and trauma identification using various soft computing techniques. This goal will be realized through the following objectives

1. System level design: In this stage, we'll be using existing techniques in related areas as building blocks to design our system. A facial expression recognition system usually consists of multiple components, each of which is responsible for one task. We first need to review the literature and decide the overall architecture of our system, i.e., how many modules it has, the responsibility of each of them and how they should cooperate with each other. Implement and test various techniques for each module and find the best combination by comparing their accuracy and robustness.

2. Algorithm Level design: Focus on the classifier which is the core of a recognition system, trying to use the algorithms which hopefully have better performance for both Facial expression recognition and trauma identification
3. Overall the designed system should have the advantages as follows:

- Expression analysis and recognition done in more conducive manner
- Computationally efficient and simple.
- Reduction in feature vector dimension and reduction in computational time
- Work equally well for low resolution as well as for good quality / high resolution images
- High recognition rate

1.9 SCOPE

- Uses the databases available for research work
- Taken nearly 260 images for testing and training from JAFFE and PICS database
- Uses 2D images
- Can detect six emotions such as happy, anger, fear, neutral, sad, disgust
- Based on facial expression the emotions are identified
- Female database is considered

2.8 Summary

The current paper therefore aims to provide a better estimate of the frequency of impaired facial affect recognition in people with Trauma presenting to rehabilitation services. To do this, we examined studies presents a survey on different facial recognition techniques that uses different machine learning strategies to improve the facial recognition patterns over various applications.

THREE
DIMENSION MEASUREMENT

3.1 GENERAL

The term dimension relates to be a mathematical figure expressed in units of linear measurement of areas and objects. It facilitates planning and designing almost everything that augurs to be built or manufactured. The first step in the process of the emotion detection requires to preprocess the collected images in terms of removing the noise and the second step follows to decide on the facial region that need to be used for extracting the featuressuitable for a given task.

The extraction of the features enables to handle the "Curse of Dimensionality", and avoid issues like over-fitting in the high dimensional space. Although a vast array of algorithms remain in vogue for each module of face recognition systems, how to combine them still exists to be a challenging problem, especially for an expression recognition task and where ambiguity becomes an essential issue to be faced.

The facial expressions and the associated changes provide important information about the effective state of the person, his temperament and personality, psychopathological diagnostic information, information related to stress levels and truthfulness. The body language and facial expression constitute to be the best ways to know the personality of a person and the response of a person in various situations.

The study involves a person's face for feature extraction and the dimension measurement because face owes to be one of the strongest indicators of the emotion. The face of the speaker contributes 55% to the effect of the spoken message and allows sharingthe social information with others and communicates both verbally and non-verbally. The facial expressions basically encompass to be movements of the numerous muscles supplied by the facial nerve that remain attached to and move the facial skin.

3.2 PROBLEM DEFINITION

The primary emphasis owes to measure the dimension of the chosen image from an inclusive data set with a purpose to either identify or detect the influence of emotion and trauma. It involves extracting features that relate to the image under study using an appropriate choice of the existing methods which include the DCT, Gabor filter, PCA, ICA, LDA and processing the Image among others and in turn classify them in order to calculate the dimensions in terms of area, perimeter, solidity, orientation, Centroid, major and minor access length in the MATLAB platform.

3.3 PROPOSED METHODOLOGY

The approach engages the preprocessing of the image and extracting the features, instead of directly giving the features as the input to the classifiers here the dimension of extracted features are measured and then it is given as input to the classifier, because it will produce best matching between the input and the output data because of the normal human facial structure with reduced feature vector dimension, which in reduces the computational complexity.

3.3.1 Feature Extraction

The flow diagram in the Fig. 3.1.enables to detect the human face features from the original image by removing the neck and part of hair. It necessitates cropping the image to form the input to the image enhancement unit. It carries out contrast adjustment and performs Gamma correction with a gamma value of 1.25. A Gamma value greater than 1 expands the lighter regions and compresses the darker regions of the original image and facilitates the facial features of the images to stand out. The removal of hair a mask originates from the preprocessed image by converting the image into black and white and removing smaller structures.

The exercise of converting the image into black and white and complementing the result of the preprocessed image serves to extract the enhanced image and ANDing the mask with the enhanced image provides the facial features with their orientation and size.

The procedure extracts the eyes, mouth and eyebrows as the extracted features and determines their geometrical dimensional parameters that include the area, orientation, perimeter, solidity, major axis length, minor axis length and centroid. As the centroidbears x and y values, it creates a total of 40 features (eight geometrical features of five facial features (two eyes, two eyebrows and mouth)) for each image.

a. Original Image (b) Cropped Image (c) Preprocessed Image

(d) Mask (e) Enhanced Image (f) Facial Features

Fig. 3.4 Outputs of feature extraction steps

The Fig. 3.4 depicts the outputs of the feature extraction steps and classifies the facial features that include the change in the shape and size of eyebrows, eyes and lips into different expressions. The eyes mouth the parameters that include the area, orientation, perimeter, solidity, major axis length, Minor Axis Length; Centroid(x, y axis) as shown in the Figs.3.5 and 3.6 as a result there arrives 8 parameters, with 5 features for each image.

Fig. 3.5 Values to be Measured

**Fig. 3.6(a) Values of Measurements for
18 images(training data)with different emotions**

**Fig. 3.6(b) Values of Measurements for 18 images
(training data)with different emotions**

Fig 3.3 (a)Testing data for 25 images

Fig 3.3(b) Testing data for another 25 images

Fig 3.4(a)Testing data for 25 images

Fig. 3.5(b) Testing data for another 25 images

3.4IMAGE DATASET

The images obtained from the online public resource available on the internet: JAFFE (Japanese Female Facial Expression) create the database that contains 10 unique females, each one of which includes 18 poses for 6 different expressions. It formsa total number of 180 expressions for each pose in each female whose emotions require to be recognized. The Fig. 3.1 shows the sample images and the Table 3.1 explains the details of the total of 180 images.

The Trauma recognition the same system uses the database PICS (Psychological Image Collection at Stirling) with 63 images and 7 expressions for a total of 9 females. The Table 3.2 shows the total of 81 images with 6 different expressions posed by 9 different females for Trauma recognition.

Fig. 3.2Samples of dataset images from JAFFE

Fig. 3.3 Sample Images Database from PICS Table 3.1The JAFFE dataset images

Facial Expression

No. of Expression per Females

Facial Expression	No. of Expression per Females	No. of poses per expression	Number of females
Happy	6	18	10
Sad	6	18	10
Anger	6	18	10
Neutral	6	18	10
Disgust	6	18	10
Fear	6	18	10
Total	**6**	**180**	**10**

Table 3.2 PICS dataset

Facial Expression	No. of Expression per Females	No. of poses per expression	Number of females
Happy	7	9	9
Sad	7		
Anger	7		
Neutral	7		
Disgust			
Fear			
Trauma			

	7
	7
	7
	9
	9
	9
	9
	9
	9
	9
	9
	9
	9
	9
	9
Total	
	7
	81
	9

3.5 SUMMARY

The basics and the importance of the dimensional measurement have been brought out. The measurements that invite attention in the perspective of the image analysis have been explained. The details of the data set have been presented exclusively for both recognizing the expressions and the trauma identification.

FOUR

Emotion identification using FFNN and RNN

4.1 INTRODUCTION

The emotion recognition appears to be interesting research work because emotions play an important role in fostering smoother communication. It finds its use spread across different fields that cover medicine, E-learning, monitoring, marketing, entertainment and law.

The philosophy of emotion gathers to be a strong feeling derived from one's circumstances, mood or relationships with others. The link between the emotion felt by an individual and the facial expression they display turns out to be both reflexive and reflective. However the expressions continue to be generally accepted as the primary observable response.

The shortest route to investigating the human emotion cuts directly through the field of facial expression research. Naturally the human emotions augur to be an area of great interest for many practical applications, rendering facial expressions research to be a popular field.

A facial expression relates to be one or more position of the muscles beneath the skin of the face. According to one set of controversial theories the movements convey the emotional state of an individual to observers. The facial expression engages to be a form of non verbal communication to translate primarily social message between humans.

Among the classification techniques the Neural Network (NN) finds an extensive role in accomplishing emotion recognition. The study offers an overview of the face detection and expression recognition using artificial neural network (ANN) with aim to provide recent holistic and feature based approaches (Nisha et al(2015)).The use of eyes and lip as biometric elements for face emotion recognition (Mehdi Akhari Oskuyee (2012)) open up a new dimension in this perspective.The emergence of feed forward neural network (Deepthi.S et al (2013)) enables to increase accuracy in face emotion recognition.

4.2 Problem Definition

The focus orients torecognize facial expression based on the extracted features through the use of intelligent techniques that include FFNN and RNN. The exercise avails the use of the data sets gathered for the purpose and attempts to use the dimensions measured in the previous chapter as inputs. It assuages to examine the performance on the MATLAB platform and estimate the accuracy of the results in terms of the metrics.

4.3 Proposed Methodology

The emotions can be recognized through different modalities that include speech, facial expression and body gestures. The emotion recognition through facial expression invite attention in the last few decades and the expression of the face convey a lot without speaking.

According to Hyisung C. Hwang and David Matsumoto (2016) the human emotion can be delineated into two major ways that include indirect approaches which involve **observer judgments** of produced facial expressions, where in the emotions of the expressors remain inferred through the obtained judgments. The second being the direct measurement of the facial muscle movements owes to classify the observed facial configurations as emotional expressions (or other types of classifications) based on a taxonomy or dictionary of sorts.

The last step of AFEA (Automatic Facial Expression Analysis) systems alleges to recognize the facial expression using FFNN and RNN for classification of different emotions in the form of being Happy, Sad, Anger, Neutral, Afraid And Disgusted.

The automatic facial expression recognition system explained through the schematic in the Fig. 4.1 operates using image processing and artificial neural networks.The geometrical features extracted for different classes of expression form the training input – target class pair to the neural network.

It attempts to test the system with the jaffe image dataset and estimate the performance using the parameters that include confusion matrix, error histogram, mean absolute error(MAE), error plot and regression plot, accuracy, sensitivity, specificity, precision.

On measuring the various dimensions, it classifies the values with FFNN and RNN.

Step 1: The system implements the FFNN with the BPN algorithm and the network performance tested in the lower end at epochs 100 and another in the higher end at epochs 1000.

Step 2: It evaluates the performance using the confusion matrix, the error plot, the error histogram, the regression Plot, the target Vs output Plotand the indices that include the accuracy,specificity, sensitivity, precision and the mean absoluter error (MAE),

Step 3: Since the results indicate that the FFNN doesnot work well with the BPN, it leaves way for the implementation of FFNN with BRBPN algorithm.

Step 4: Owing to the fact that the FFNN doesnot work well with BRBPN as well it introduces the RNN with BPN algorithm and thereafter it decides to settle down to operate using RNN the BRBPN algorithm.

The Feed Forward neural network undergoes a process of training with the Backpropagation algorithm through the following steps.

Step 0: Initialize weights

Step 1: While Stopping Condition is False, do Steps 2 to 9

Step2: For each training pair, do steps 3-8

Feed forward

Step 3: Input receives input signal and propagates it to all units in the hidden layer

Step 4: Each hidden unit sums its weighted input signals

Step 5: Each output unit sums its weighted input signals and applied its activation function to compare its output signal

Step 6: Each output unit receives a target pattern corresponding to the input training pattern, computes its error information term

X_i – input units i=1 to n

Z_j – Hidden units j=1 to p

Y_k – output units k=1 to m

V_{ij} – weights on connection between input and hidden layer

V_{oj} – bias on input unit j

W_{jk} – weights on connection between hidden and output layer

W_{ok} – bias on output unit k

$d_k=(T_k - Y_k)f'(Y_{ink})$ (4.1)

It calculates its bais correction term from Eqns. (4.2) and (4.3)

$DW_{jk}=\alpha d_k Z_j$ (4.2)

$DW_{ok}=\alpha d_k$ (4.3)

and sends d_k to the units in the layer below

Step 7:Each hidden unit sums its delta inputs

as in Eqn. (4.4)

$d_{inj}=Sd_k*W_{jk}$ (4.4)

It multiplies by the derivative of its

activation function to calculate error information as

in Eqn. (4.5)

$d_j=d_{inj}*f'(Z_{inj})$ (4.5)

and calculates its weight correction term

from the Eqn. (4.6)

$DW_{jk}=\alpha d_k Z_j$ (4.6)

the bias correction term using (4.7)

$DW_{ok}=\alpha d_k$ (4.7)

Update weights and biases

Step 8: Each output unit updates its bias and weights as in Eqn.(4.8)

$W_{jk}(new)=W_{jk}(old) + DW_{jk}$ (4.8)

Each hidden unit updates its bias and weights as in Eqn. (4.9)

$V_{ij}(new) = V_{ij}(old) + DV_{ij}$ (4.9)

Step 9: Test Stopping condition

4.4 PERFORMANCE EVALUATION OF FFNN WITH BPN

The exercise creates the architecture of the FFNN and RNN with 40 inputs nodes20 hidden nodes and one output node and operates using hperbolic tan-sigmoid activation function in hidden layer and the Linear activation function at the output layer. The procedure follows the same structure for both BPN and BRBPN algorithms. The FFNN and RNN however use Linear Activation function at the output layer.

The network with the FFNN-BPN algorithm converges at 8 epochs and the training stops because the validation vectors effect stop training early if the network performance on the validation vectors fails to improve or remains the same in the max_fail epochs in a row. The test vectors offer to serve as a further check in order that the network generalizes and does not have any effect on the training.

The confusion matrix can be used to assess the performance of a classifier where the off-diagonal elements represent the misclassified data. A good classifier yields a confusion matrix that look to be dominantly diagonal with(Angry (A), Disgust(B), Fear(C), Happy(D), Neutral (E) and Sad(F).The diagonal of the matrix calculates to be 1 for extracting the system to be ideal in its performance.

The procedure wrongly identifies expression A as Disgust, Fear and Happyupto 50% with minimum number of epochs 8 and for the expression B upto 80% correctly and wrongly misclassifies as Fear upto 20%. It identifies the expression C upto 70.6% correctly and incorrectly upto 23.5 % as Disgust and 5.9% as Happy.It relates the expression D correctly upto 61.5% and the remaining percentage wrongly as Anger, Fear, Neutral and Sad. It predicts the Neutral(E) correctly upto 68.8% and wrongly to a certain percentage as Disgust, Fear, Happy and Sad, and the expression E correctly upto 76.5% and misclassifies as Fear and Happy upto 17.6% and 5%respectively as shown in the Fig. 4.2.

The error plot shows the error at each instant of time and varies from -3 to 3 for 8 epochs as seen from the Fig. 4.3. The error plot of horizontal line from zero (from error axis) indicates the good system prediction capabilityfor the FFNN system. However the output using FFNN with BPN algorithm as noticed in the Fig. 4.5 doesn't give the horizontal line, which indicates the networks poor prediction capability.

The plot drawn between the system outputs and actual classesin the Fig. 4.4 expresses the regression between them and further brings out that the regression value of 1 indicates perfect fit.

The expression for the output can be expressed as in the Eqn. 4.18

Output =0.8^target+0.72 (4.18)

With achosen target value it becomes possible to get a pretty good estimate of the emotion for any expression. For example (Angry(1), Disgusted(2), Fear(3), Happy(4), Neutral(5), Sad(6)), the output=0.8*3+0.72 =3.12 which falls close to the target for the Fear expression. The regression value from the graph turns out to be as 0.85885 to establish the credibility of the model.

Inputs and targets are data we are using to train net. Inputs and targets are correct data that is known. After trainingthe network, by sending again only inputs, and the output would be predicted based on inputs and targets you have sent in training session. So the targets should be the correct output for data.

The target refers to the correct or decided value for the response associated to one input and usually on comparison with the output response of the NN, it serves to guide the learning process involving changes in the weight.A perfect matching between the target and the output plot exhibits to show that the network works efficiently as a good classifier. The Fig. 4.5 in any case infers that the FFNN with BPN algorithm doesn't work as efficiently in identifying the expression.

The dispersion of the system errors depicts the error histogram plot as a measure of the anomalies. The anomalies owe to be the data points where the fit between the original and the target class becomes significantly worse than the majority of data. The error histogram of the FFNN system in the Fig. 4.6 reveals that the maximum errors fall near the zero range, with the error span from -2.85 to 2.85 to show that it recognizes wrongly certain expressions.

The procedure evaluates the performance of the FFNN with BPN at the lower end through a histogram. The first step requires creating a bin (or bucket) for the range of values by dividing the entire range of values into a series of intervals. The Bins relate to the number of vertical bars on the graph and the error from the NN ranges from -2.85(Leftmost bin) to 2.85(Rightmost bin). The error range on being divided into 20 smaller bins, so each bin spaces a width of (2.85-(-2.85))/20=0.285

Each vertical bar represents the number of samples from our dataset which lies in a particular bin for example at the mid of the graph, there exists a bin corresponding to the error -0.15 and the height of that bin for validation dataset appears to be nearly 10, to show that 10 percentage of the samples from the validation dataset find the error to lie in the following range.

(-0.15-0.285/2, -0.15+0.285/2) = (-0.2925,-0.0075) which represents the range of the bin corresponding to -0.15 and allows the error histogram to claim a good ability to predict when only the errors lie distributed within a reasonably good range around zero. The entries in the Table.4.1 summarize the performance of the FFNN with the BON algorithm through well defined parametric metrics.

Table 4.1 Performance Measures of FFNNusing BackpropagationAlgorithm with the Number of Epochs 8

S.No	Parameters	Epochs 8	Descriptions
1.	MAE	0.47	Incorrect Identification. Ideal value is zero
1.	Accuracy	0.68	Closeness of identification to original expression of a class and identification of expression not belonging to the same class. Ideal value is 1. The value of 0.68 shows the system having poor precision capability
3.	Precision	0.65	Consistency of Prediction. Ideal value is 1. The value of 0.65 shows the system having poor precision capability
4.	Specificity	0.97	Correct identification of objects not belonging to a class Ideal value is 1. Pretty close the ideal value which indicates the system is having good specificity
5.	Sensitivity	0.11	Correct identification of objects belonging to a class Ideal value is 1. The value of 0.11 shows the system is having very poor sensitivity.

The sensitivity predicts one category(object belonging to the class) and the specificity(object not belonging to the class) predicts another category. Where ever accuracy measures the networks predicting capability, both categories(object belonging to the class and object not belonging to the class) do play a role. Therefore if both sensitivity and specificity become high,the accuracy may be high but if both fall low the accuracy turn out to be low.

It becomes important to note that when specificity turns out to be higher, the accuracy varies with specificity. Similarly when the network enables to identify the object belonging to the class(higher sensitivity), then it follows that the accuracy varies with sensitivity without considering specificity.

The sensitivity follows to be the degree of awareness and the responsiveness to changes/ability to respond to changes.

4.5PERFORMANCE EVALUATION OF FFNN WITH BRBPN ALGORITHM

The number of epochs runs properly at both lower end and upper end, so it shows comparison of the performance of FFNN-BR algorithm for epochs 100 and 1000.

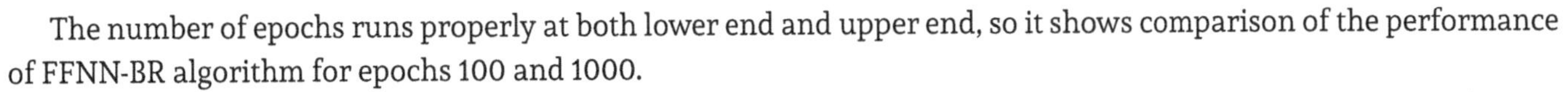

Fig. 4.7Confusion Matrix for Emotion Identification using FFNN-BRBPN with 100 Epochs

Fig. 4.8Confusion Matrix for Emotion Identification using FFNN-BRBPN with 1000 Epochs

For Epochs 100: The expression A (Anger) has been identified upto 27.8 % and 33% it has been identified as sad and upto to 38.9% it has been identified as Fear. And for the expression B(Disgust) it has been correctly identified upto 33% and wrongly identified as 60.7% as Fear and upto 6.7% it has been identified as Happy. And the expression C has been identified upto 52.9% correctly and it has misclassified as Sad and Happyof upto 17.6% and 23.5% and upto 5% as Neutral. And the expression D (Happy) has been identified upto53.8% has been identified correctly andmisclassified upto 46.8% as Disgust, Fear, Sad. And the expression E (Neutral) has been identified correctly upto 31.3% and misclassified upto 68.8 as Happy and Neutral. And the expression F (Sad) has been correctly identifiedupto 11.8% and misclassification wasupto 17.6% as anger,29.4 % for Happy and upto 41.2% as Neutral as shown in Fig. 4.7.

Epochs 1000: The expression A has been identified upto 94.4 % correctly and it has been wrongly identified upto 5% as Fear. And the expression B has been identified correctly upto 86.7% and the misclassification is upto 13.3% as Fear. And the expression C has been identified upto 82.4% correctly and it has been misclassified has Disgust, Happy, Neutral of upto 17.7% and the expression D has been idenified correctly to upto 92.3 % and it has been misclassified as 7.7 % as Sad. And expression E has been identified correctly for the percentage of 93.8% and it has been wrongly identified as fear for upto 6% and similarly for Sad the correct classification is upto 82.4% and the misclassification of upto 17.7% as Fear, Happy, and Neutral as shown in Fig. 4.8.

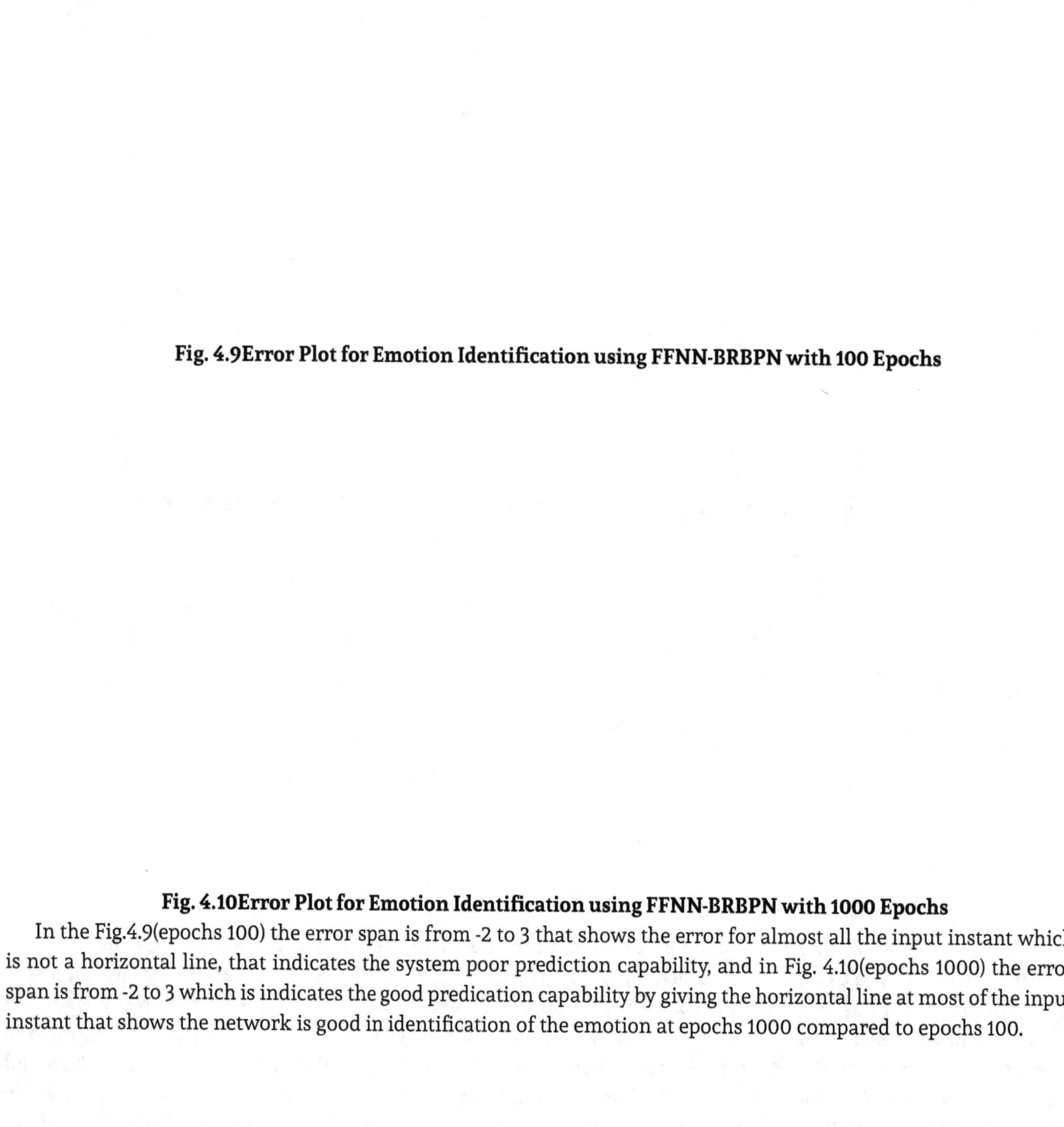

Fig. 4.9Error Plot for Emotion Identification using FFNN-BRBPN with 100 Epochs

Fig. 4.10Error Plot for Emotion Identification using FFNN-BRBPN with 1000 Epochs

In the Fig.4.9(epochs 100) the error span is from -2 to 3 that shows the error for almost all the input instant which is not a horizontal line, that indicates the system poor prediction capability, and in Fig. 4.10(epochs 1000) the error span is from -2 to 3 which is indicates the good predication capability by giving the horizontal line at most of the input instant that shows the network is good in identification of the emotion at epochs 1000 compared to epochs 100.

Fig. 4.11Regression Plot for Emotion Identification using FFNN-BRBPN with 100 Epochs

Fig. 4.12Regression Plot for Emotion Identification using FFNN-BRBPN with 1000 Epochs

The regression gives the R value which for this graph shown in fig 4.11as 0.74196 which is fairly a decent model and by still increasing the number of epochs to 1000 shown in fig. 4.12the R value becomes 0.94121 that shows the system is very good increase in performance. But for this methodology the ideal value of R should be equal to 1. The output from best of all equation can be calculated by assigning the target can be calculated similarly as given in section 4.5.3.

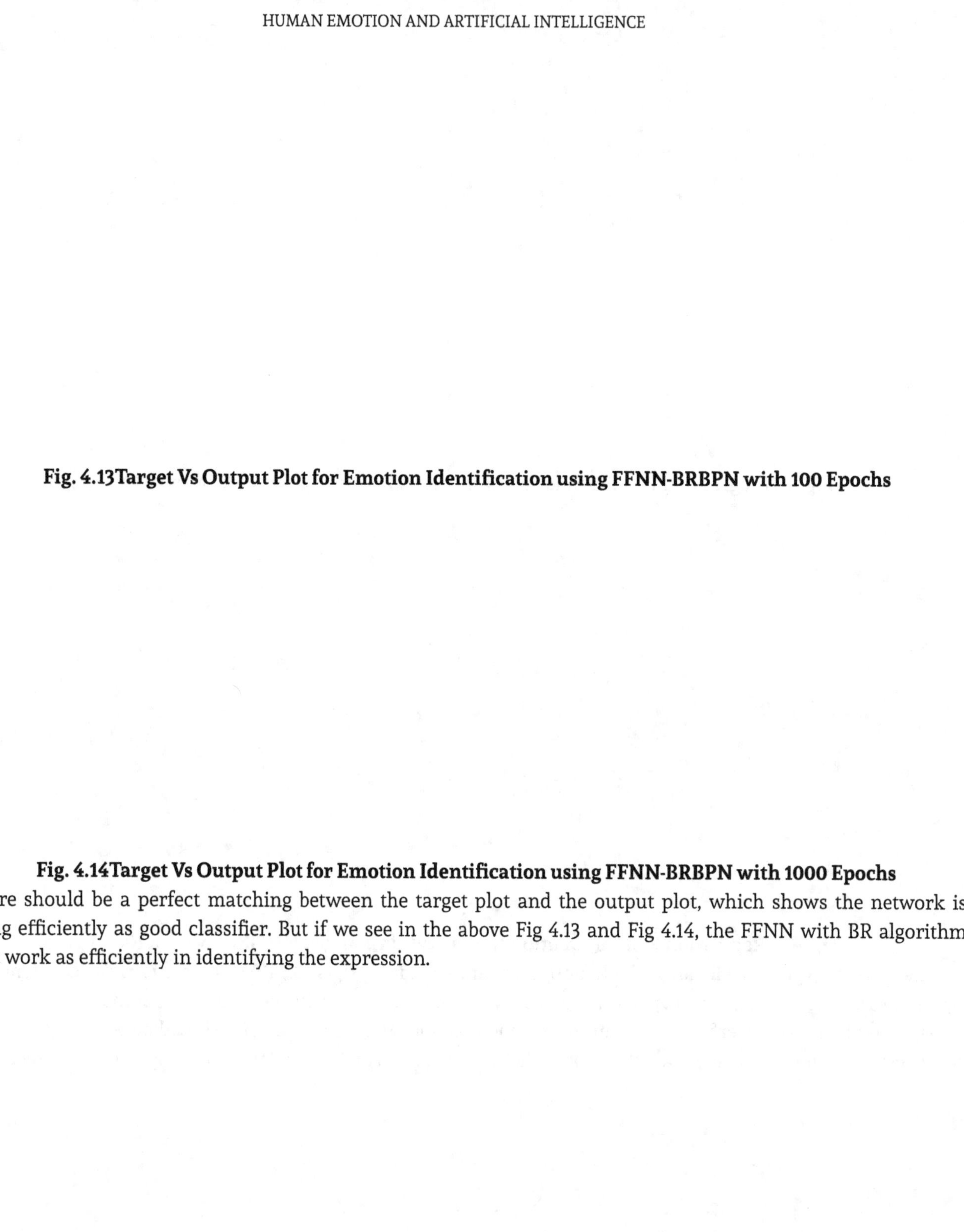

Fig. 4.13Target Vs Output Plot for Emotion Identification using FFNN-BRBPN with 100 Epochs

Fig. 4.14Target Vs Output Plot for Emotion Identification using FFNN-BRBPN with 1000 Epochs

There should be a perfect matching between the target plot and the output plot, which shows the network is working efficiently as good classifier. But if we see in the above Fig 4.13 and Fig 4.14, the FFNN with BR algorithm doesn't work as efficiently in identifying the expression.

Fig. 4.15Error Histogram for Emotion Identification using FFNN-BRBPN with 100 Epochs

Fig. 4.16Error Histogram for Emotion Identification using FFNN-BRBPN with 1000 Epochs

Error Histogram of FFNN with BR Algorithm with 100 epochs Shown in Fig. 4.15:

When the number of epochs is 100 the error histogram shows around 35 % of the samples are good range nearby zero, and some of the error lie out of the zero range which needs the betterment in network performance.

Error Histogram of FFNN with BR Algorithm with 1000 epochs shown in Fig. 4.16:

When we the increase the number of epochs to 1000 the error histogram shows an increase in the prediction ability of the system most the samples lie in the good range i.e., nearby zero. And there are also some samples which need to be identified further. But maximum error falls near zero which indicates betterment in the system performance. Approximately 90% of the samples are good range nearby zero. And the error range for each instance can be calculated similarly as given in section 4.5.1.

Table 4.2 Performance Evaluation of FFNN with BR Algorithm for the Epochs 100 and 1000

S.No	Parameters	Epochs 100	Epochs 1000	Descriptions
1	MAE	0.88	0.18	
2	Accuracy	0.78	0.96	

For epochs 100 the value 0.88 shows the higher range of error when compared with the ideal value of 0. But for epochs 1000 the MAE value is nearby zero range which shows the betterment in network performance when increasing the number of epochs. Which naturally justifies the idea of varying the number of epochs performs well in this work.

Here for epochs 100 the accuracy is upto 0.78 which is somewhat closer to the ideal value of 1, but of the epochs 1000 the value of 0.96 shows the range which is very much close to the range of ideal value. But for epochs 100 the sensitivity is very low and specificity is good so explained earlier accuracy can be considered fair only when both sensitivity and specificity are high or low so for epochs 100 accuracy of 0.78 is considered as an unfair value and for epochs 1000 both sensitivity and specificity is high so accuracy can be considered as an fair value and the system works good with this range of epochs.

3

Precision

0.29

0.88

Similarly the precision here shown here for epochs 100 shows the poor precision capability and for epochs 1000 it shows a fairly a decent value of 0.88 which is nearby the range of the ideal value 1.

4

Specificity

0.86

0.97

The network is have good specificity value for both 100 epochs and 1000 epochs which is nearby the range of ideal value 1.

5

Sensitivity

0.33

0.88

The system is highly sensitive at epochs 1000 and it shows a poor sensitivity for epochs 100

4.6 PERFORMANCE EVALUATION OF RNN WITH VARYING NUMBER OF EPOCHS WITH BPN ALGORITHM

Fig. 4.17 Confusion Matrix for Emotion Identification using RNN-BPN with 100 Epochs

Fig. 4.18Confusion Matrix for Emotion Identification using RNN-BPN with 1000 Epochs

The performance of a classifier is better evaluated by the confusion matrix. It is an error matrix portrayed by a table layout which helps in visualizing the performance of classifier. The columns of the confusion matrix represent the instances in the output class whereas the rows represent the instances in the actual class.

For Epochs 100: The expression Happy A has been identified correctly upto 27.8% and for the expression Sad B the correct recognition rate was upto 46.7% and for the expression Fear C the correct recognition rate was upto 47.1% and for expression D i.e., Happy the correct recognition rate was upto 53.8% and for the expression Neural the correct recognition rate was upto 53.8% and for the expression F the correct recognition rate was upto 29.4%. And the numbers which is present other than diagonal indicates the misclassification rate of each and every expression, for example the expression A i.e., Angry has been misclassified as Disgust and Fear of upto 44% and 27.8% which is shown in Fig. 4.17.

For Epochs 1000: The expression A has been identified upto 83.3% and the expression B has been identified 100% and C has been identified upto 94.1% and the 92.3% accuracy in identifying the expression Happy and Neutral E has been identified upto 81.3% and the sad F has been identified upto 76.5% and this shows that when we increase the number of epochs the system performance too increases which is shown in Fig. 4.18.

Fig. 4.19Error Plot for Emotion Identification using RNN-BPN with 100 Epochs

Fig. 4.20Error Plot for Emotion Identification using RNN-BPN with 1000 Epochs

In Fig. 4.19 (for epochs 100) the error span is from -2 to 3 which doesn't give the horizontal line at all which indicates that is a occurrence of error at every input instant and in Fig. 4.20 (epochs 1000) the error span is from -1 to 1 and it can be seen that horizontal line at some input instant which indicates the systems good performance for some of the input instance.

Fig. 4.21Regression Plot for Emotion Identification using RNN-BPN with 100 Epochs

Fig. 4.22 **Regression Plot for Emotion Identification using RNN-BPN with 1000 Epochs**

For epochs 100 (Fig. 4.21) R value for this graph is 0.83744 shows the network prediction capability and if by still increasing the number of epochs 1000 (Fig. 4.22) i.e., the R value becomes 0.97983 for epochs 1000 which is almost equal to 1.

Fig. 4.23 **Target Vs Output Plot for Emotion Identification using RNN-BPN with 100 Epochs**

Fig. 4.24Target Vs Output Plot for Emotion Identification using RNN-BPN with 1000 Epochs

There should be a perfect matching between the target plot and the output plot, which shows the network is working efficiently as good classifier. But if we see in the above Fig. 4.23 and Fig. 4.24, the RNN with BPN algorithm doesn't work as efficiently in identifying the expression, so we are going to use BR algorithm in the place of BPNalgorithm with the same network (i.e., RNN)

Fig. 4.25Error Histogram for Emotion Identification using RNN-BPN with 100 Epochs

Fig. 4.26Error Histogram for Emotion Identification using RNN-BPN with 1000 Epochs

For epochs 100: When the number of epochsis 100 the error histogram given in Fig 4.25 is around 40 % of the samples are good range nearby zero. And also shows that most of the samples falls out of the zero range which need to be identified further.

For epochs 1000: When the increase the number of epochs to 1000(shown in Fig. 4.26) the error histogram shows an increase in the prediction ability of the system most the samples lie in the good range i.e., nearby zero. And there are also some samples which need to be identified further. But maximum error falls near zero which indicates betterment in the system performance. Approximately 90% of the samples are good range nearby zero. Section 4.2.1

gives the error range calculation for each bin.

Table 4.3: Performance evaluation of RNN with BPN algorithm for the epochs 100 and 1000

Parameters	Epochs 100	Epochs 1000	Description
MAE	0.67	0.12	System performance is good at epochs 1000 which is almost nearby the ideal value 0. But it is poor at epochs 100
Accuracy	0.81	0.95	System performance is good at both cases but at epochs 1000 the value is very much close to the ideal value 1. But for epochs 100 it is an unfair value because of lower sensitivity.
Precision	0.39	0.86	Among both values, the precision of 0.86 at epochs 1000 shows the system is more precise and works good in identification of emotion
Specificity	0.88	0.97	The system has good specificity in both the cases and by increasing the number of epochs from 100 to 1000 the system becomes more specific.
Sensitivity	0.44	0.87	The network works good with higher sensitivity for epochs 1000.

4.7 PERFORMANCE EVALUATION OF RNN WITH VARYING NUMBER OF EPOCHS WITH BR ALGORITHM FOR EMOTION DETECTION

Fig. 4.27Confusion Matrix for Emotion Identification using RNN-BR with 100 Epochs

Fig. 4.28Confusion Matrix for Emotion Identification using RNN-BR with 1000 Epochs

For Epochs 100

The diagonal element of the confusion matrix shown in Fig. 4.27 gives the correct identification rate i.e., the expression A has been identified upto 44% correctly and the expression B has been identified upto 73.3% and the expression C has been correctly identified upto 70.6% and the expression D has been correctly identified upto 69.2% and the expression E has correctly identified upto 50% and the expression F has been identified upto 47.1%. Here the maximum correct identification has been given for only expression B and C i.e., Disgust and Fear with more than 50% of correct identification.

For Epochs 1000

In confusion matrix shown in Fig. 4.28 gives the diagonal element of 1 indicates the perfect identification all the expression and here for the RNN system with the BR algorithm shows the perfect identification all the expression.

Fig. 4.29Error Plot for Emotion Identification using RNN-BR with 100 Epochs

Fig. 4.30Error Plot for Emotion Identification using RNN-BR with 1000 Epochs

Error plot is the plot between error and the input instant. It shows the error at each instant of time. For FFNN system the error plot is shown in Fig.4.29. The error varies from -2 to 2 with epochs 100 as shown in Fig. 4.31and in Fig. 4.30 (epochs 1000) horizontal line at zero (from error axis) indicates the good system prediction capability.

Fig. 4.31Regression Plot for Emotion Identification using RNN-BR with 100 Epochs

Fig. 4.32Regression Plot for Emotion Identification using RNN-BR with 1000 Epochs

The regression plot is drawn between the system outputs and actual classes. It shows the regression between them. The R value of 1 indicates perfect fit. That might be good enough, but regression also gives us a useful equation, which for this chart is of epochs 100 as shown in Fig. 4.31.

Output = 0.75*Target+0.9 (4.19)

What that means is we can plug in a Target value and get a pretty good estimate of the emotion for any expression. For example (Angry(1), Disgusted(2), Fear(3), Happy(4), Neutral(5), Sad(6)), 3: output=0.75*3+0.9= 3.15which is pretty close to 3 for the fear expression but not exactly 3. Best of all, we can use this equation to make predictions. The regression also gives us the R value which for this graph is 0.91227 which shows the system fairly decent and we can be fairly confident in our emotion prediction for the epochs 100 and if we are going to still increase the number of epochs the performance i.e., the R value becomes 1 for epochs 1000. Similarly the regression equation for epochs 1000 as shown in Fig. 4.32,

Output= 1*Target+1.3e-1.6=1*3+1.3e-1.6=3 (4.20)

This is exactly equal to 3 which indicate the perfect identification of Fear expression.

Fig. 4.33Target Vs Output Plot for Emotion Identification using RNN-BR with 100 Epochs

Fig. 4.34Target Vs Output Plot for Emotion Identification using RNN-BR with 1000 Epochs

There should be a perfect matching between the target plot and the output plot, which shows (Fig. 4.34) that for the epoch's 1000 network is working efficiently as good classifier. But in the Fig. 4.33 plot of epochs 100, the RNN with BR algorithm doesn't work as efficiently in identifying the expression.

Fig. 4.35Error Histogram for Emotion Identification using RNN-BR with 100 Epochs

Fig. 4.36 Error Histogram for Emotion Identification using RNN-BR with 1000 Epochs

The dispersion of the system errors is depicted by the error histogram plot. This histogram is a measure of anomalies. The anomalies are the data points where fit between the original class and the target class significantly worse than the majority of data. The error histogram of RNN with BR algorithm is shown in above Figs. 4.35 and 4.36. In this case it can be seen that for the epochs 1000 the maximum errors fall near the zero range and we can also see there is no error other than that in the entire range of error span which is from -0.96 to 0.96which shows most of the expressions has been identified properly for the epochs 1000upto 98% (approximately), which is shows the greater improvement than the FFNN using BPN and BR algorithm.

Table 4.4 Performance evaluation of RNN with BPN algorithm for the epochs 100 and 1000

S.No

Parameters

Epochs 100

Epochs 1000

Description

1.

MAE

0.45

0

Incorrect Identification for epochs 100. Ideal value is zero has been achieved for epochs 1000

2.

Accuracy

0.86

1

Closeness of identification to original expression of a class and identification of expression not belonging to the same class. Ideal value is 1 has been achieved for epochs 1000 and for epochs 100 the accuracy shows an unfair value because of lower sensitivity.

3.

Precision

0.54

1

Ideal value is 1 and it has achieved for epochs 1000

4.

specificity

0.91

1

Correct identification of objects not belonging to a class Ideal value is 1.

5.

sensitivity

0.57

1

Correct identification of objects belonging to a class Ideal value is 1.

Table 4.5 shows FFNN with BR algorithm, RNN with BP algorithm is somewhat near to the ideal values but not equal to it, and the performance of RNN with BR by the network performance becomes ideal and works good at higher end i.e., for 1000 epochs .

4.6 SUMMARY

This chapter dealt with the performance evaluation of FFNN and RNN with varying number of epochs and varying the algorithm and it shows that RNN-BR algorithm gives perfect identification of emotion at epochs 1000 with the BR algorithm

FIVE

EMOTION IDENTIFICATION WITH ANFIS USING THE CONCEPT OF ANOVA

CHAPTER 5

5.1 INTRODUCTION

The process of identifying emotions gathers significance in view of the emerging challenges that include among others the need to relate among a group of different people who work under different environments. It further embodies a framework to distinguish between people involved in a variety of satires and may enable them to bring out the best from them.

The intelligent techniques appear to hold the key in the sense they provide means of articulating ways to operate in the data sets and serve to identify the emotions through well defined categories. The Neuro-fuzzy techniques that evolve as the fusion of the Artificial Neural Networks (ANN) and the Fuzzy Inference Systems (FIS) offer a wide scope in the attempt to reach out to the theory of identification.

An Adaptive Neuro Fuzzy Inference System (Jang et al.), in which a polynomial is used as the defuzzifier and the structure commonly referred to as ANF1S exhibit a scheme that can be used in the identification process. The ANFIS differs from the normal fuzzy logic systems by the adaptive premise and the consequent parameters. It basically operates as fuzzy Sugenomodelswithin the framework of adaptive systems to facilitate learning and adaptation. It allows the Fuzzy Logic Controller to be more systematic and less relying on expert knowledge.

The ANFIS finds an extensive role in the worksthat achieve emotion recognition rate of 90%-95% (Anagha S. Dhavalikar et al., (2014)),ANFIS and NN with 30 test samples to accomplish a recognition rate upto 97.142% (S.P. Kahandit et al.,(2012) The paper uses facial geometry algorithm propagation neural network (BPNN) and (ANFIS) for ED by using the JAFFE database. Another significant contribution arises with trained and untrained images to register recognition of 94.7%. using ANFIS (Swathi Mishra, Avinash Dhole et al., (2016))

However with issues and challenges continuing to spring there exists a need to still further improve on the efficiency in identifying emotion and assuage it to suit to different areas of study.

5.2 Problem Definition

The philosophy relates to identify the emotions of the human kind through the use of the data sets gathered with typical cases. It starts with a need to measure the dimensions of the images and thereafter charter a mechanism to classify them using as ANFIS as a tool. Owing to the inert fact that ANFIS requires a larger number of rules for the specified number of twenty four inputs, it becomes necessary to reduce the number of inputs to four by the concept of ANOVA. The investigation augurs the use of the FFNN and RNN and arriving at identifying the traumatic state with the reduced number of inputs and evaluate the performance through the same metrics. The procedure encompasses to work on the MATLAB portal and illustrate its merits over the earlier approach in terms of the defined metrics.

5.3 Proposed Methodology

The emotionidentification Using ANFIS-Sugeno Model engages the Triangular Membership Function with the reduced number of inputs (No. of inputs reduced from 40 to 4) and uses the concept of ANOVA (Analysis of Variance). It is given to FFNN and RNN and tested for its performance in emotion identification as shown in Fig. 5.2.

The main concept behind the use of ANOVArelates to the rejection of null hypothesis, in the sense if the means of the different classes remain the same (null hypothesis), then it can be said that there exists no significant difference between the class else it creates a significant difference.

The variance between the four different classes may be due to the significant difference in texture between them or may be random and insignificant texture differences. But the variance within the class may be due to random and/or insignificant texture differences only. Hence dividing the between class variance by within the class variance results yields the F ratio in Eqn. (5.1) that arises due to the significant texture difference only.

$$F = Variance between the classes Variance within the class \qquad (5.1)$$

It becomes interesting to note that if the variance, calculated through the sum of squared distances within the class remains small, then statistically the same small value in variance between the classes may be sufficient to yield significant result.

The Fuzzy Logic requires fuzzy rules and the number of fuzzy rules relates to be equal to the product of the number of the membership functions (MFs) in each input variable. Owing to the fact that the ANFIS allows to change the parameters of the MFs, the time taken for training becomes directly proportional to the number of the input variables.

With the Triangular membership function and 40 inputs, the number of rules created becomes equal to ($3^{\wedge}40 = 12157665459005693000$).Therefore with higher number of inputs, the ANFIS requires a larger time to determine the output. Besides the increase in the number of rules may create problems in terms of running out of memoryand thus the approach invites the concept of ANOVAfor reducing the number of inputs and there from finding out the emotions.

The endeavor orients to examine the network performance with lower value of epochs 3and the results show that the ANFIS can produce better output at epochs 3 itself. Howeveron FFNN and RNNbeing implemented with the concept of ANOVA as shown in Fig. 5.3, it produces poorer outputs both in the lower and higher end.

The following outline the theory on which it operates the algorithm.

1 Give the 40 inputs to ANFIS for FFNN and RNN

2. MATLAB runs out of memory

3. So the number of inputs need to reduced for ANFIS for working in MATLAB

4. Implement the concept of ANOVA

5. Number of inputs reduces from 40 to 4

6. Now 4 inputs enter the ANFIS with triangular membership function

7. The exercise finds that while giving 100 epochs, an early stopping occurs and the ANFIS stops training at 3 epochs to avoid overfitting problem, for the reduced number of inputs obtained using ANOVA.

8. The ANFIS works better with 3 epochs itself and hence acquires the output at epochs 3 to achieve 100% accuracy in the identification of the emotion.

9. On implementing the FFNN and RNNwith both 40 and 4 inputs, it does not succeed in identifying the emotions.

The difference in the number of samples in each class affects the variance calculation and the Mean Squares (MS) serves to calculate the magnitude of inter and intra class variations.

$$MSb = Vbd-1 \qquad (5.2)$$

$$MSw = Vwf-d \qquad (5.3)$$

Where MSb in the Eqn. (5.2) refers to the between class variance measure, MSw in the Eqn. (5.3) refers to the within class variance measure and d, the number of classes, f, the total number of samples. d-1 and f-d, the degrees of freedom. It refers to the number of ways in which the variability in the given sample can be estimated. The Fcrit valueF can be written as in the Eqn. (5.4) from the F-Table in accordance with the number of degrees of freedom in the numerator and denominator of the F ratio.

$$F = MSbMSw \qquad (5.4)$$

The Sum of the Squares (SS) refers to the sum of the squared deviations from the meanvalue P, which indicates the measure of arriving at this accuracy by pure chance, despite the absence of substantive difference. The lower the p-value, the better seems to be the chance of null hypothesis rejection.

The idea owes to reduce the number of the input variables based on their variance in the group of input variables. If the p value becomes smaller than the significance level, it indicates that at least one of the sample means (indirectly variance) remain significantly different from the others.

The Figs.5.4(a) and 5.4(b) show (20, 7,15,1) to be the choice for the four parameters based on the least p value and follows that the 20th parameter accrues the least p value. It benign the least variance with 7th parameter, the 7th parameter accords the least variance with the 15th parameter and the 15th parameter least with the 1st parameter.

The procedure operates the four inputs with the triangular membership function on the Sugeno model as shown in Fig.5.6, allowing the number of rules to reduce to 3^4=81 and follow the process of training, with a requisite to validate the test inputs. The entries in the Table 5.1 include the framework in terms of the specifications and the ideal values of the parametric indices.

(a)

(b)

Fig.5.4 (a) and (b) After Implementing ANOVA, the Number of Inputs gets reducedto 4

Fig. 5.6: Validating the Network with Test Input
Table 5.1 Performance Framework For ANFIS
Performance Evaluation
Emotion Detection

No. of Inputs
4
Algorithm
Backpropagation
Membership Function
Trimf
Transfer Function
Hyperbolic Tan Sigmoid
Error Histogram
Nearly 100% of value lies near the zero line
which indicates the perfect identification of the emotions.

Error Plot

Zero error

Regression Plot

R=1(indicate the perfect fit)

Confusion matrix

Diagonal entries relate to correct identification of the expressions

Specificity

1

Sensitivity

1

Accuracy

1

Precision

1

Mean Absolute Error

0

5.4PERFORMANCE EVALUATION OF ANFIS FOR EMOTION IDENTIFICATION

Fig. 5.7 Confusion Matrix of ANFIS for Emotion Identification

The confusion matrix, an error matrix portrayed by a table layout helps in visualizing the performance of the classifier. The columns of the confusion matrix represent the instances in the output class whereas the rows represent the instances in the actual class. The Fig. 5.7 shows the confusion matrix obtained through the use of the ANFIS, where in the entries of the diagonal and off –diagonal matrix become 1 and 0 respectively to reflect the exact identification of the expressions.

Fig. 5.8 Error Plot of ANFIS for Emotion Identification

Fig. 5.9 Regression Plot of ANFIS for Emotion Identification

The error plot of ANFIS in Fig. 5.8 follows a horizontal line to indicate the zero error for all the inputs.The plot drawn between the system outputs and the actual classes for the regression value of 1 indicates perfect fit for training, testing and validation for the entire data as seen from the Fig. 5.9.The plot may be generalized to follow the Eqn. (5.5)

Output =1*target+1.3e-16 (5.5)

It indicates that one can plug in the target value and get a pretty good estimate of the emotion for any expression. For example with Angry(1), Disgust(2), Fear(3), Happy(4), Neutral(5), and Sad(6), the output=1*3+1.3e-16= 3 becomes exactly equal to the target and the regression value as seen from the graph shows to be 1, explaining it to be a perfect model.

Fig. 5.10 Target Vs Output Plot of ANFIS for Emotion Identification

The target relates to be the correct or the decided value for the response associated to the input and on comparison with the output, it enables the response of the neural network to guide the learning process involving the weight changes.

The network shows the perfect matching between the target and the output plot, which reveals that the network works efficiently as good classifier as seen from the Fig. 5.10.

Fig.5.11 Error Histogram of ANFIS for Emotion Identification

It can be seen fromthe Fig. 5.11that the maximum errors fall between -0.15 and 0.05, in the sense the error for entire input falls within this span which indicates that the network correctly recognizes the expressions.

The total error from the neural network ranges from -0.95(Leftmost bin) to 0.95(Rightmost bin) and shows that almost 100 percent of the data sample for facial expression identification lies near the zero range which indicates that the efficiency of the system in identifying the given emotion. The error range being divided into 20 smaller bins, so each bin occupies a width of (0.95-(-0.95))/20=0.095.

Each vertical bar represents the number of samples from the dataset which lies in a particular bin for example, at the mid of our graph, there exists a bin corresponding to the error -0.05 and the height of that bin for validation dataset turns out to be 100. It means that nearly 100 samples from the validation dataset accrue errors to lie in the following range.

(-0.05-0.095/2, -0.05+0.095/2)

(-0.0975,-0.0025) < Range of the bin corresponding to -0.05

The error histogram confirms the system to enjoy the ability to predict when only the errors remain distributed within a reasonably good range around zero. The entries in the Table. 5.2 relate to the description of the effects of the parametric indices, obtained using ANFIS.

Table 5.2 Performance Evaluation of ANFIS for Emotion Identification

S.No	Parameters	ANFIS- emotion	Description
1.	Accuracy	1	Idea Value of 1 has been achieved. Which shows the greater accuracy in detecting the emotion
2.	Precision	1	Idea Value of 1 has been achieved.
3.	Sensitivity	1	Idea Value of 1 has been achieved.
4.	Specificity	1	Idea Value of 1 has been achieved.
5.	MAE	0	Shows the perfect identification of emotion by giving the ideal value of zero for MAE

The above Table 5.2 shows the ideal value of 1 for accuracy, precision, sensitivity, specificity which indicates that the ANFIS is working better in identifying the emotion at the lower end itself.

5.5 PERFORMANCE EVALUATION OF FFNN-BPN WITH ANOVA

The effort orients to test the performance of the FFNN and the RNNwith the concept of ANOVA to check how it performs when the number of inputs reduces to 4 from 40 inputs.The confusion matrix, with the rows and columns corresponding to the true and the predicted class respectively displays the total number of observations in each cell. The Fig.5.12shows that none of the diagonal elements extracts the output value as 1 to indicate the incorrect identification of the expression.

It identifies Anger(A) upto 44.4%, Disgust(B) upto 20%, Fearupto 41.2%, Happy(D) upto 46.2%, the Neutral(E) recognized with 43.8% and the Sad(F) exactly upto 5.9%.

Fig. 5.12 Confusion Matrixof FFNN-BPN with the concept of ANOVA for identifying emotion

Fig. 5.13 Error Plotof FFNN-BPNwith the concept of ANOVA for Identifying Emotion

The error plot of horizontal line at zero (from error axis) indicates good system prediction capability, but with the error varying from -3 to 4in the Fig.5.13 shows error at every input instant and ends up poor system prediction capability. The plot in the Fig 5.14 with the regression value of 0.599 for the FFNN-BPN along with ANOVA further justifies the poor prediction capability.

Fig. 5.14 Regression Plotof FFNN-BPNwith the concept of ANOVA for Identifying Emotion

Fig. 5.15 Target Vs Output Plotof FFNN-BPN with the Concept of ANOVA for Identifying Emotion

Thegraph drawn between the target and the output plot in the Fig. 5.15 adds to the cause of theFFNN with BPN algorithmand ANOVAnot being able to efficiently identify the expression.The total error from the neural network ranges from -2.825(Leftmost bin) to 3.825(Rightmost bin) and the Fig. 5.16 shows that nearly 35 percent of the samples lie near the zero range and about 65 percentage of instances lie out of the zero range.

The entries in the Table. 5.3 comprehend the performance of the FFNN with BPN and ANOVA in terms of the parametric indices for different epochs.

Fig. 5.16Error Histogram of FFNN-BPN with the concept of ANOVA for identifying emotion

Table 5.3: Performance Evaluation of FFNN with BPNAlgorithm for the Epochs 8 with ANOVA

Parameters

Epochs 8

Description

Mean Absolute error

1.062

Incorrect Identification. Ideal value is zero

Accuracy

0.78

This accuracy is considered as an unfair value because of lower sensitivity

Precision

0.29

The network shows the poor precision value compared to the ideal value of 1

Specificity

0.86

Correct identification of objects not belonging to a class. Ideal value is 1. The network shows the good specificity value

Sensitivity

0.3318

The network is less sensitive for the given input

5.6 PERFORMANCE EVALUATION OF FFNN-BR WITH ANOVA

Fig. 5.17 Confusion Matrix for 100 epochs of FFNN-BR with the Concept of ANOVA for Identifying Emotion

Fig. 5.18 Confusion Matrix for 1000 epochs ofFFNN-BR with theConcept of ANOVA forIdentifying Emotion

The emotions have been mostly misidentified as Fear and Happy in both. The confusion matrix while it correctly identifies fear upto maximum of 35.3%, 47.1% for 100 epochs and 1000 epochs in the Figs 5.17 and 5.18 respectively, the percentage for the emotion Happygoes upto 92.3% in the higher level.

Fig. 5.19 Error Plot for 100 Epochs of FFNN-BR with theConcept of ANOVA forIdentifying Emotion

Fig. 5.20 Error Plot for 1000 Epochs ofFFNN-BR with theConcept of ANOVA forIdentifying Emotion

The error plot of horizontal line at zero (from error axis) indicates the good system prediction capability for both 100 and 1000 with the error span from -3 to 3 in the Figs 5.19 and 5.20 respectively.

The expression for this condition with 100 epochs from the Fig. 5.21 follows the Eqn. (5. 6)

Output = 0.061*Target+3.5 (5.6)

With a target of 3 the equation becomes output=0.061*3+3.5= 3.683 which falls pretty close to 4 and indicates the Happy expression. But the given target relates to Fear (3) and since the output does not align with the target, the plot gives the regression value as 0.209, which does not correspond to the ideal value of 1.

Similarly for 1000 epochs 1000, the Fig. 5.22 gives the output expression to read as in the Eqn. (5.7)

Output= 0.059*Target+3.4=0.059*3+.4=3.577 (5.7)

It yields a value almost equal to 4, shows the output not being equal to the target and gives the regression value of 0.21 to exhibit the poor prediction capability.

Fig. 5.21 Regression Plot for 100 epochs of FFNN-BR with theConcept of ANOVA forIdentifying Emotion

Fig. 5.22 Regression Plot for 1000 Epochs ofFFNN-BR with the concept of ANOVA forIdentifying Emotion

Fig. 5.23 Target Vs Output plot for 100 epochs ofFFNN-BR with theConcept of ANOVA forIdentifying Emotion

Fig. 5.24 Target Vs Output Plot for 1000 epochs ofFFNN-BR with theConcept of ANOVA forIdentifying Emotion

Fig. 5.25 Error Histogram for 100 epochs of FFNN-BR with the concept of ANOVA for identifying emotion

Fig. 5.26 Error Histogram for 1000 epochs of FFNN-BR with theConcept of ANOVA forIdentifying Emotion

Both the plots in the Figs. 5.25 and 5.26 show that only nearly 20% of the sample falls near the zero range and the other values lies out of the zero range to again establish the poor prediction capability after implementing the concept of ANOVA. The description in the Table. 5.4summarize the performance of the FFNN with BR algorithm through the parametric indices for both 100 and 1000 epochs.

Table 5.4 Performance evaluation of FFNN with BR algorithm for the epochs 100 and 1000 with ANOVA

S.No	Parameter	Epochs 100	Epochs 1000	Description
1.	MAE	1.44	1.43	Here the error value is shown greater than the ideal value which shows the network doesn't work well with this concept of ANOVA
2.	Accuracy	0.73	0.74	No improvement in network performance when increasing the number of epochs also. And also the accuracy value shown here is an unfair value because of its lower sensitivity.
3.	Precision	0.187	0.20	The network shows the poor precision value
4.	specificity	0.83	0.84	The network is having good specificity
5.	Sensitivity			

0.185

0.19

There is no improvement in sensitivity when increasing the number of epochs from 100 to 1000 also. At both the conditions the network shows the poor sensitivity.

5.7 PERFORMANCE EVALUATION OF RNN-BPNWITH ANOVA

Fig. 5.27 Confusion Matrix for 100 Epochs of RNN-BPN with the Concept of ANOVA for Identifying Emotion

Fig. 5.28 Confusion Matrix for 1000 Epochs of RNN-BPN with the Concept of ANOVA for Identifying Emotion

While the diagonal elements of the confusion matrix in the Fig. 5.27 represent the number of points for which the predicted label becomes equal to the true label, the off-diagonal elements relate to those mislabeled by the classifier for 100 epochs. It follows that the higher the diagonal values the better the predictions being correct.

The results show that the network does not perform well because it identifies only the expressions Anger, Neutral, Sad (A,E,F) correctly and offers to pick on the expression like Disgust(B), Fear(C), Happy(D) only upto 13.3%,41.2%,61.5%.

The results in the Fig. 5.28 with epochs 1000 identifies Anger correctly upto 5.6%, the Disgust upto 20%, the Fear correctly upto 47.1%, the Happy upto 53.8%, the Neutral identified upto 25% and the network does not identify Sad.

Fig. 5.29 Error Plot for 100 Epochs ofRNN-BPNwith theConcept of ANOVA forIdentifying Emotion

Fig. 5.30 Error Plot for 1000 epochs ofRNN-BPNwith theConcept of ANOVA forIdentifying Emotion

The Figs. 5.29 and 5.30 with the error span from -3 to 3for 100 and 1000 epochs respectively do not show a horizontal line at any instance and thus can be inferred that the RNN-BPN doesn't work well with the concept of ANOVA.

The Eqn. (5.8) gives the expression the output for 100 epochs from the Fig. 5.31 for an assumed target of 3 to give a value of 3.43 and a regression value of 0.3075.

Output =0.11*target+3.1=0.11*3+3.1=3.43 (5.8)

Output= 0.25*Target+2.6=0.25*3+2.6=3.35 (5.9)

Similarly for epochs 1000 the output from the Fig. 5.32 follows the Eqn. (5.9) and offers an output value of 3.35 and allows the regression value to increase to 0.47173. Howeverthe output does not exactly equal to the target, gives a poor regression value and a poor prediction capability.

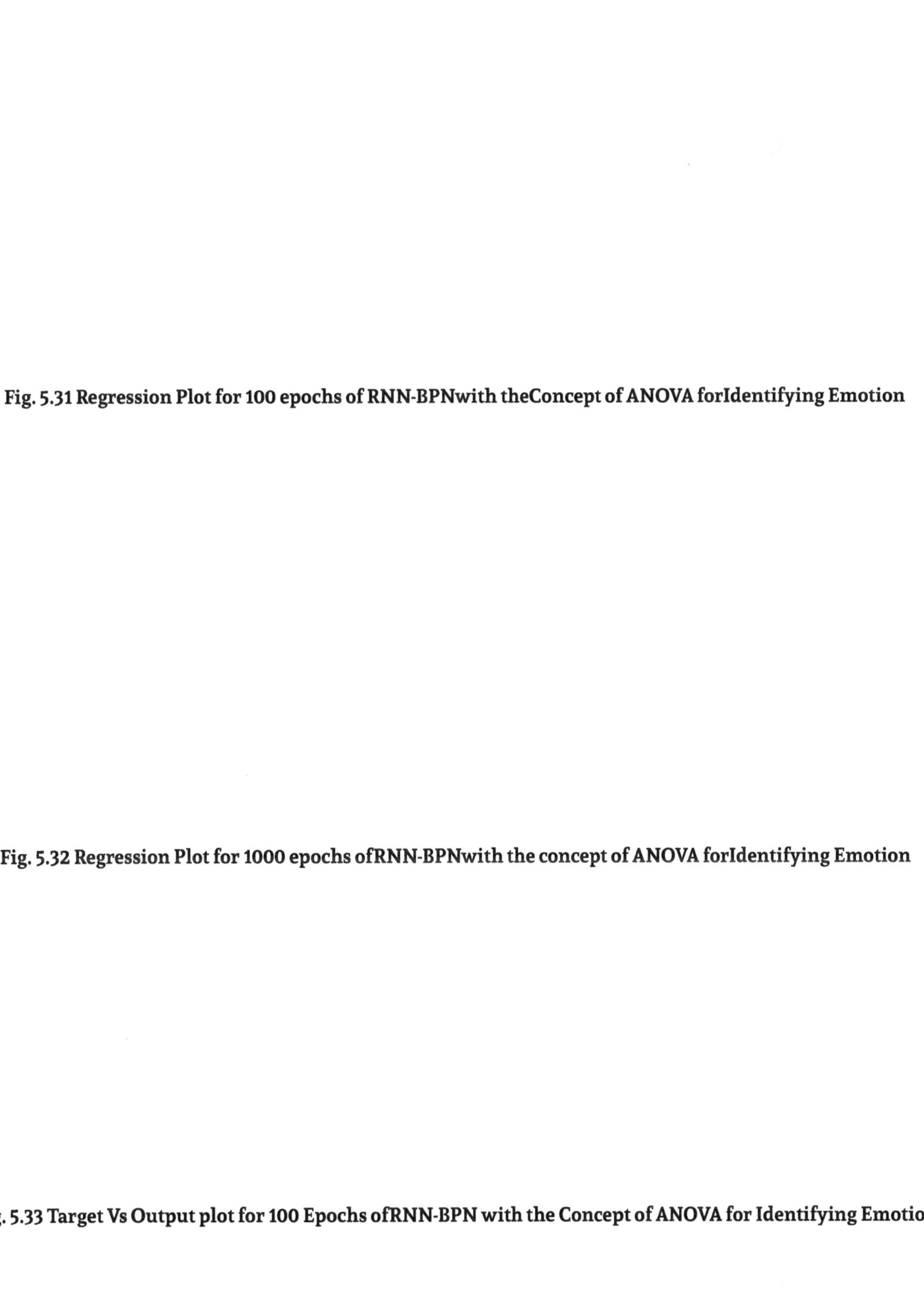

Fig. 5.31 Regression Plot for 100 epochs of RNN-BPNwith theConcept of ANOVA forIdentifying Emotion

Fig. 5.32 Regression Plot for 1000 epochs ofRNN-BPNwith the concept of ANOVA forIdentifying Emotion

Fig. 5.33 Target Vs Output plot for 100 Epochs ofRNN-BPN with the Concept of ANOVA for Identifying Emotion

Fig. 5.34 Target Vs Output Plot for 1000 Epochs of RNN-BPN with the Concept of ANOVA for Identifying Emotion

The RNN with BPN algorithm doesn't work as efficiently in identifying the expression asseen from the graph in Figs. 5.33 and 5.34.Both the graphs in the Figs. 5.35 and 5.36 shows only nearly 15% of the sample falls near the zero range and the majority of the values lie out of the zero range to reflect the poor prediction capability for epochs 100. Howeverfor epochs 1000 nearly 25% of the data falls in zero range, while the other data's falls beyond the zero range to show the in correct identification of the emotions.

The readings in the Table 5.5 comprehend the description of the performance of the network through the indices for both 100 and 1000 epochs.

Fig. 5.35 Error Histogram for 100 Epochs of RNN-BPN with theConcept of ANOVA forIdentifying Emotion

Fig. 5.36 Error Histogram for 1000 Epochs ofRNN-BPN with the concept of ANOVA for identifying emotion

Table 5.5 Performance Evaluation of RNN with BPNAlgorithm for the Epochs 100 and 1000 with ANOVA

Parameters	Epochs 100	Epochs 1000	Description
MAE	1.42	1.23	The error value for this case, it goes beyond the ideal value, which indicates the network could not identify any of the emotion
Accuracy	0.72	0.75	This accuracy is considered as an unfair value because of lower sensitivity.
Precision	0.16	0.22	The network is showing very poor precision values
Specificity	0.83	0.85	The system is having good specificity values
sensitivity	0.16	0.23	The network is having poor sensitivity

5.8 PERFORMANCE EVALUATION OF RNN-BR WITH ANOVA

Fig. 5.38 Confusion Matrix for 100 epochs of RNN-BR with the Concept of ANOVA for Identifying Emotion

Fig. 5.39 Confusion Matrix for 1000 epochs of RNN-BR with the concept of ANOVA for Identifying Emotion

The confusion matrix identifies Fear correctly upto maximum of 70.6% for 100 as seen in the Fig. 5.38 and Happyupto 64.7% for 1000 epochs as noticed from the Fig. 5.39.The error plot shown in theFigs. 5.40and 5.41 for 100 and 1000 epochs respectively with the span from -3 to 3 shows the error at every input instant and no where the horizontal line appears.

The expression in the Fig.5.42 for 100 epochs follows the Eqn. (5.10) assuming a target of 3 to yield aoutput value of 3.323 and a regression value of 0.1486.

Output $=0.041*target+3.2= 0.041*3+3.2= 3.323$ (5.10)

The expression in the Fig. 5.43 follows the Eqn. (5.11) for 1000 epochs with a target equal to 3 to result in an output value of 3.359 and a regression value of 0.117601.

Output$= 0.053*Target+3.2=0.053*3+3.2=3.359$ (5.11)

Both the cases indicate that the output does not become exactly equal to the target and extracts a poor regression value almost nearer to the zero range.

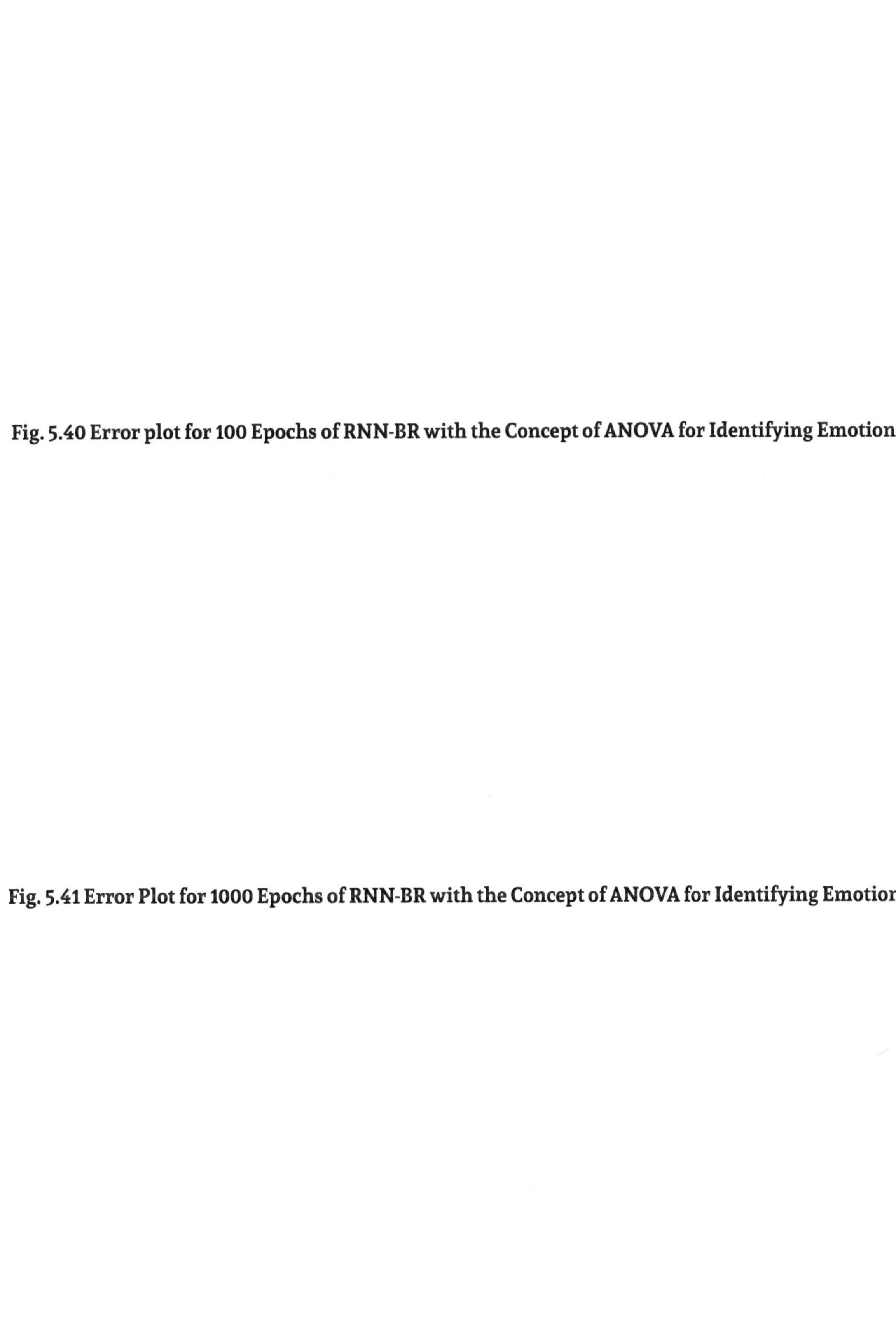

Fig. 5.40 Error plot for 100 Epochs of RNN-BR with the Concept of ANOVA for Identifying Emotion

Fig. 5.41 Error Plot for 1000 Epochs of RNN-BR with the Concept of ANOVA for Identifying Emotion

Fig. 5.42 Regression Plot for 100 Epochs of RNN-BR with theConcept of ANOVA forIdentifying Emotion

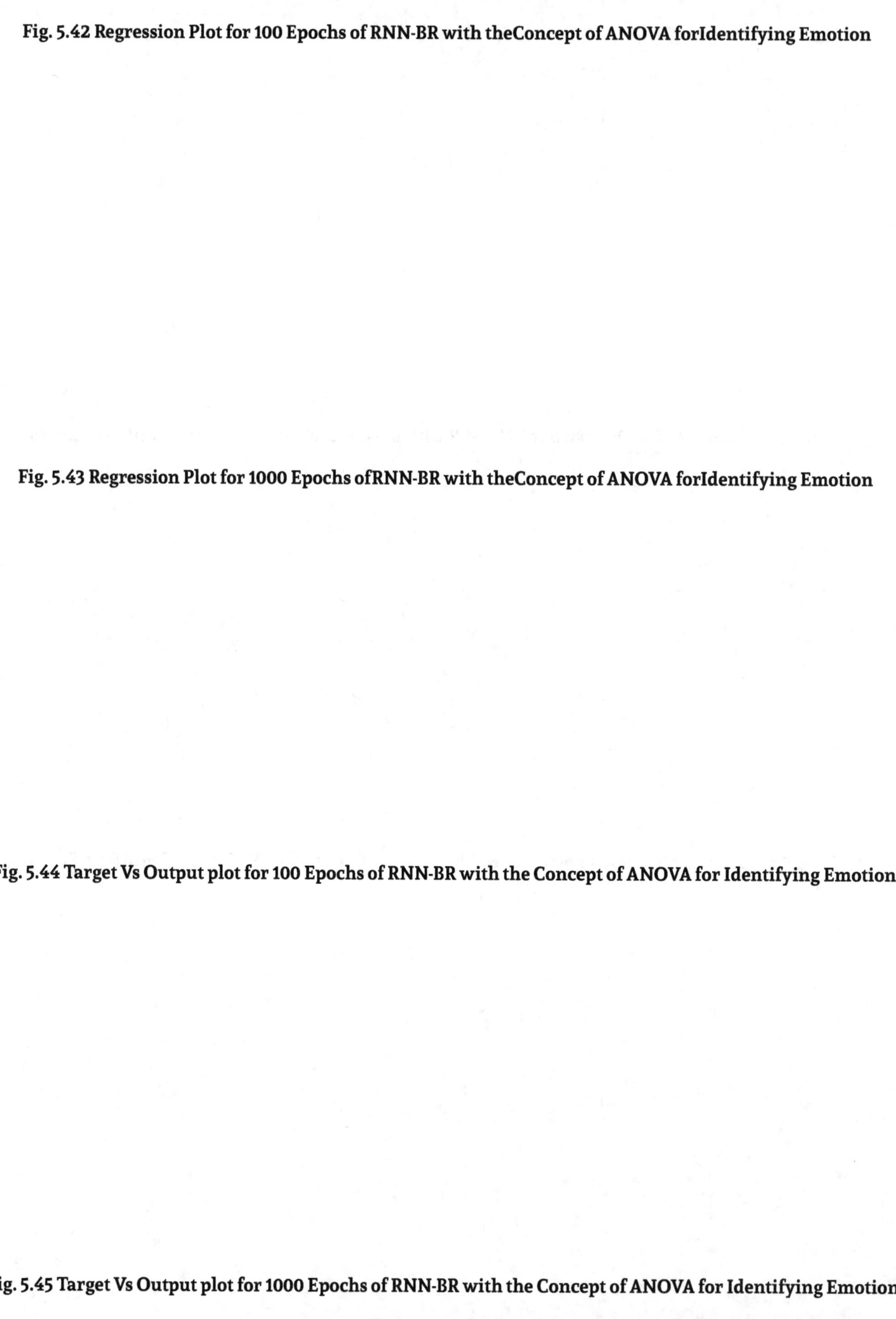

Fig. 5.43 Regression Plot for 1000 Epochs ofRNN-BR with theConcept of ANOVA forIdentifying Emotion

Fig. 5.44 Target Vs Output plot for 100 Epochs of RNN-BR with the Concept of ANOVA for Identifying Emotion

Fig. 5.45 Target Vs Output plot for 1000 Epochs of RNN-BR with the Concept of ANOVA for Identifying Emotion

Fig. 5.46 Error Histogram for 100 epochs of RNN-BR with the concept of ANOVA for identifying emotion

Fig. 5.47 Error Histogram for 1000 epochs of RNN-BR with theConcept of ANOVA for Identifying Emotion

The target output plot in the Figs 5.44 and 5.45 show that the network does not working efficiently in the identification of the emotion for both the epochs.

The error histogram graph in the Figs. 5.46 and 5.47 for both 100 and 1000 epochs indicate that only 20% of the data lies in the zero range and the other data samples lie outside the zero range to show the in correct identification of the expressions. The Table 5.6includes the description relating to the performance of the network in terms of the indices.

The Table. 5.7 compares the performance of the different types of networks used along with the chosen algorithms. It brings out that ANFIS works out to extract the best results over the others.

Table 5.6 Performance Evaluation of RNN with BPNAlgorithm for the Epochs 100 and 1000 with ANOVA

Parameter	Epochs 100	Epochs 1000	Descriptions
MAE	1.46	1.45	The error value for this case, it goes beyond the ideal value, which indicates the network could not identify any of the emotion
Accuracy	0.73	0.73	

Both the for epochs 100 and 1000 the network shows the lower prediction capability and this accuracy value 0.73 is mainly because of the dependency of specificity and accuracy will be considered as the fair value only when both specificity and sensitivity as higher or lower. If any one is lower and other is higher means the accuracy is considered as an unfair value.

Precision

0.20

0.20

The network is showing very poor precision values

Specificity

0.84

0.84

The system is having good specificity values

Sensitivity

0.19

0.20

The network is having poor sensitivity

Third network dealt in this work is ANFIS and it uses the concept of ANOVA and its performance is shown in the Table 5.1, we have tested the other two network performance by implementing the same concept ANOVA(i.e., with the reduced number of inputs) and we conclude from the above Table 5.7that FFNN with BPN, BR algorithm and RNN with BPN, BR algorithm doesn't work good, and it has the poor prediction capability.

5.9 SUMMARY

The emphasis has been enticed to identify the emotion of a person in the framework of ANFIS, the FFNN and RNNthrough BPN and BR algorithm with the concept of ANOVA. The investigations have been carried out for both 100 and 1000 epochs and the performance studied using the parametric indices that include Error histogram, Error Plot, Confusion Matrix, Mean Absolute Error, target Vs output plot, specificity, sensitivity, accuracy and precision. The results have been elaborated to follow the chosen ideal values for distinguishing between the correct and incorrect classifications. It has been projected that ANFIS with the concept of ANOVA churns out the correct identification of the emotions.

SIX

TRAUMA IDENTIFICATION USINGFFNN AND RNN

6.1 INTRODUCTION

The term trauma relates to a sense of psychosis and emerges from the reaction to an extreme stress that an individual may not be able to cope with. One of the prevailing effects of trauma underscores the development of post traumatic stress disorder (PSTD). It engages the physiological changes a system undergoes as a consequence of the occurrence of the incident.

The recognition of trauma includes a wide range of diagnostic measures that rely on a culmination of a host of technologies. It ranges from the basic examination in the sense allowing them to answer a set of question to the most modernCTscan (X-ray *Computed tomography*). However each of them experiences its own limitations and augurs fresh initiatives toreach out to the remedial cause.

Identifying the traumatic situation from the basic emotion identification assumes significance particularly when the person is under traumatic stress. The inside pain comes out through the face and the facial features in drastic situation or recollection. The influence of the facial expression may offer scope to identify trauma from the reflection of the emotional state of the individual. It depends on the ability to interpret the clues resulting from crucial social interaction.

There exists many ways of identifying traumatic condition of a person like by CT scan[Somayeh(2016)], MRI scan [Rayan(2017)], by Post-Trauma mobile psychology service[Zhen(2010), Yang(2009)], psychological counseling service with Mobile Internet technology[Fan Zhang(2009)], by using StartleMart[Christoffer(2016)] game and by facial feature extraction[Takeo Fujiwara(2015), GiotaStratou(2014), Caroline J. Bell(2017), Jessie(2017) Michael(2017), Ryan(2017) Carrie(2007)].

6.2 PROBLEM DEFINITION

The exercise endeavors to identify trauma through the facial expressions in the initial stage using intelligent techniques. It incites particularly to recognize the traumatic situation in case of fear and sadness from a wide variety of data sets collected for the purpose. It involves procedure to examine the performance on the MATLAB portal and bring out the results in terms of metrics.

6.3 METHODOLOGY

The sense of trauma conceives to be an experience that threatens the life more often and when the symptoms persist for longer period of time it becomes known as post traumatic stress disorder or PTSD. The Science news, a research organization from New York university suggests that trauma increases the risk for the development of both PTSD and conduct disorder.

The effort owes to identify the initial stage of trauma, which apparently lies before the PTSDusing the help of FFNN, RNN and ANFIS.The study involves the basic emotions as a base for training the FFNN, RNN and ANFIS and creates the database. It follows a threshold of 0.22 based on the target value after training (by trial and error method)and when it exceeds the threshold the state falls into a traumatic condition.

The exercise involves only a differentiation of the normal human emotion with trauma requiring the network to identify the state being either trauma or normal and does not augur a classification of six different emotions as in the previous proposed methodologies.

Fig 6.2 Features used for trauma identification and their measurements

The Figs. 6.1 and 6.2 explain the methodology and with less number of inputs in the sense that it includes three features and eight measurements totaling to twenty four inputs for each expression and follows the same extraction and dimension measurements procedure. The steps below detail the sequence of events involved in the process and the readings in the Fig. 6.3 elucidate the veracity of the identification scheme.

Step 1: 24Inputs (3 features (eyebrows, eyes and mouth)) is given to FFNN and RNN

Step 2: A threshold value of 0.22is set for both (FFNN and RNN) the network output, when the output value goes beyond the threshold of 0.22; the network identifies it as trauma.

Step 3: The output is taken at both lower end and higher end and the network fed with the combination of both Normal (here refers to the happy, anger, sad, neutral, disgust, fear) and trauma image.

Fig. 6.3Target value set by the output for each input image and the Threshold value is set based on this target value

The performance of these two network is tested insimilar to the previous Emotion detection process through Error Histogram, Error plot, Confusion Matrix, Mean Absolute Error, Regression Plot, Accuracy, Precision, Specificity, Sensitivity, Target vs. Output plot.

6.4 PERFORMANCE EVALUATION OF FFN WITH BPN ALGORITHM

Fig. 6.4 Regression Plot for Trauma Identification using FFNN-BPN with 8 Epochs

The regression plot obtained from FFNN-BPN using eight epochs, as seen in Fig. 6.4 gives the equation as "output=0.65*Target+0.019" and follows the idea that it falls to be in the traumatic condition if the target becomes more than 0.22 and in the case of non traumatic condition it remains less than 0.22.

With a target set as 0.1 in the equation produced by the regression plot turns out to be equal to 0.65*0.1+0.019=0.084 which however shows to be not equal to 0.1, thus indicating the system does not produce the exact target value. In any case the value of 0.72169 indicates the network inefficiency in identifying the emotion.

Though the horizontal line in the plot in the Fig. 6.5 depictsa zero error, owing to the fact that the error span ranges to be from -1 to +1, it shows that itdoes not produce proper identification of the emotion and trauma.

Fig. 6.5 Error plot for Trauma Identification using FFNN-BPN with 8 Epochs

Fig. 6.6 Confusion Matrix for Trauma Identification using FFNN-BPN with 8 Epochs

The confusion matrix seen in the Fig. 6.6 brings out that the network offers to perform well in identifying the normal state of the person in order that it can achieve 0.981 and the trauma being identified upto 0.667, at the value of which it reveals that the trauma condition becomes not exactly identified.

The graph in the Fig. 6.7 displays the error histogramshows that the maximum error falls near the zero line though a few errors fall beyond the zero range.The mismatch between the target plot and output plot in the Fig. 6.8 creates a sense of wrong identification and necessitates exploring still better options.

The entries in the Table.6.1 summarize the performance measures for the case of identifying the traumatic state with eight epochs in the architecture of the FFNN –BPN.

Fig. 6.7 Error Histogramfor Trauma Identification using FFNN-BPN with 8 Epochs

Fig. 6.8 Target Vs Output plot for Trauma Identification using FFNN-BPN with 8 Epochs

Table 6.1 Performance Evaluation of FFNN with BPN Algorithm for Trauma Identificationwith Epochs 8

Parameters	Epochs 8	Description
Specificity	0.98	It indicates the network is good in its specificity by have the value very closer to the ideal value of 1.
Sensitivity	0.67	The networks show the less sensitivity with the identification emotions and trauma state
Accuracy	0.93	

This accuracy is considered as an unfair value because of lower sensitivity even though the it is near by the ideal value of 1 for both the epochs 100 and 1000, which is explained in chapter 4.

Precision

0.85

The working of FFNN-BPN gives the good precision value which is nearer to the ideal value of 1

MAE

0.063

Error is almost equal to the ideal value of 0

6.5 PERFORMANCE EVALUATION OF FFNN WITH BRBPN/BR ALGORITHM

Fig. 6.9 Regression Plot for Trauma Identification using FFNN-BR with Epochs 100

Fig. 6.10 Regression Plot for Trauma Identification using FFNN-BR with Epochs 1000

The regression plot obtained from the FFNN-BPN using 100 epochs, as seen in Fig. 6.9 gives the equation as "output=0.31*Target+0.019", and enables identifying the trauma and engage the target as 0.22 or more in the sense it remains in the trauma condition when the target becomes more than 0.22 and in the case of non-traumatic condition it becomes less than 0.22.

With thetarget set as 0.1 in the equation produced by the regression plot turns out to be equal to 0.31*0.1+0.019=0.05, which however shows to be not equal to 0.1 thus indicating the system to be incapable of producing the exact target value. The regression value of 0.45177 indicates the network inefficiency in identifying the emotion and even after increasing the epochs to 1000 the value of 0.66172 indicates the network doesn't show a perfect fit between the target and the output plot. Though the horizontal line in the plot in the Fig. 6.11 depictsa zero error, owing to the fact that the error span ranges to be from -1 to +1, it does not correctly identify the state of the emotion and trauma.

Fig. 6.11 Error Plot for Trauma Identification using FFNN-BR with Epochs 100

Fig. 6.12 Error Plot for Trauma Identification using FFNN-BR with Epochs 1000

Fig. 6.13 Confusion Matrix for Trauma Identification using FFNN-BR with Epochs 100

Fig. 6.14 Confusion Matrix for Trauma Identification using FFNN-BR with Epochs 1000

With the span from -1 to 1, the horizontal line in both the Figs. 6.11 and 6.12 indicate the zero error but the presence of the horizontal line from the error axis at 0 for some of the inputs, and also peak to peak variations in error for a few cases shows the erroneous classification between the emotions and traumatic state of the person

The confusion matrix in the Fig. 6.13 with 100 epochs shows that the network identifies normal condition upto 98.1% and does not identify the trauma condition for upto 33% correctly.However on increasing the number of epochs to 1000 the rate of correct identification for normal condition goes upto 96.3% and for the trauma upto 66.7% as observed from the Fig. 6.14.

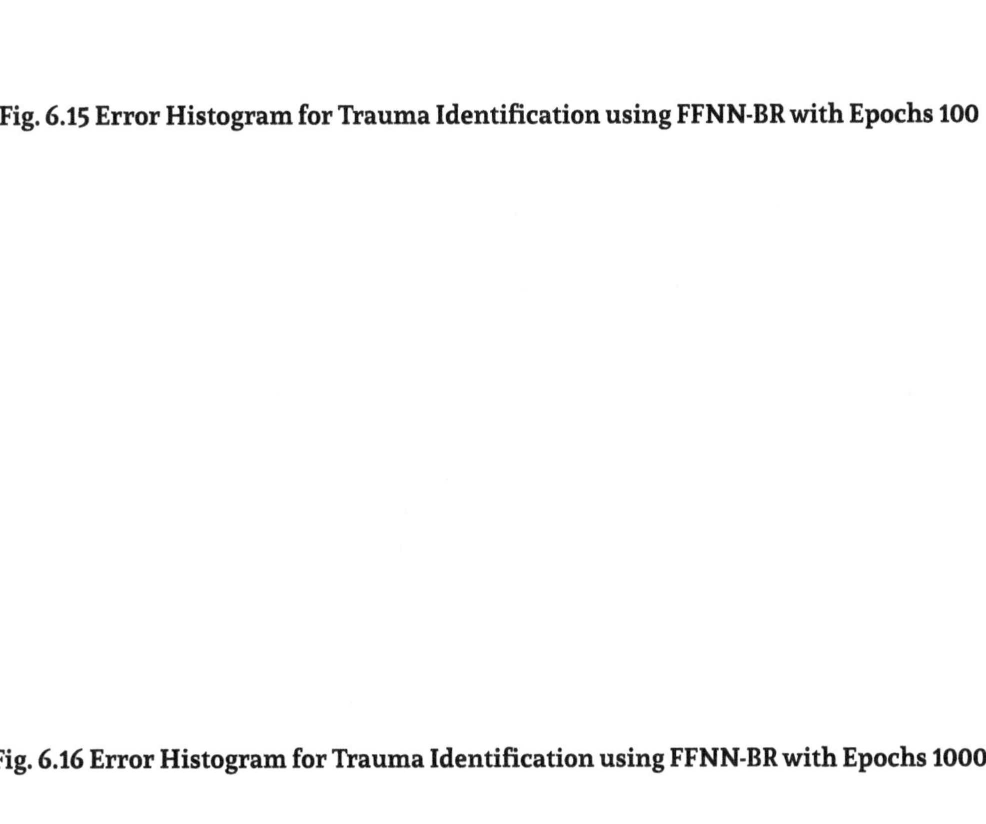

Fig. 6.15 Error Histogram for Trauma Identification using FFNN-BR with Epochs 100

Fig. 6.16 Error Histogram for Trauma Identification using FFNN-BR with Epochs 1000

Fig. 6.17 Target Vs Output Plot for Trauma Identification using FFNN-BR with Epochs 100

Fig. 6.18 Target Vs Output Plot for Trauma Identification using FFNN-BR with Epochs 1000

Though the maximum error falls near the zero range, still the existence of some error out of the zero range for both 100 and 1000 epochs indicate the improper classification of certain emotions as seen from the Figs.6 .15 and 6.16.

The imperfect matching between the target vsoutput plot for both the cases in the Figs. 6.17 and 6.18reveal the misclassification in the identification of the emotion and trauma condition. The readings in the Table.6.2 describe the classification performance of the FFNN-BR for two different epochs.

Table 6.2 Performance Evaluation of FFNN with BR Algorithm with Epochs 100 and 1000

Parameters	Epochs 100	Epochs 1000	Description
Specificity	0.98	0.96	Correct identification of objects not belonging to a class Ideal value is 1.
Sensitivity	0.33	0.66	The network shows the poor identification of objects belonging to a class when compared with the Ideal value is 1.
Accuracy	0.88	0.92	This accuracy is considered as an unfair value because of lower sensitivity even though it is near by the ideal value of 1 for both the epochs 100 and 1000.
Precision	0.75	0.75	Closeness of identification to original expression of a class and identification of expression not belonging to the same class. Ideal value is 1.
Error	0.11		

0.07

Incorrect Identification. Ideal value is zero

6.6 PERFORMANCE EVALUATION OF RNN WITH BPN ALGORITHM

Fig. 6.19 Confusion Matrix for Trauma Identification using FFNN-BR with Epochs 100

Fig. 6.20 Confusion Matrix for Trauma Identification using FFNN-BR with Epochs 1000

The confusion matrix obtained using RNN-BPN in the Fig. 6.19 with 100 epochs shows that FFNN-BR identifies the normal human emotion correctly upto 100% and the trauma only upto 33.3%, but when the epochs increase to 1000, the network performance seen in the Fig. 6.20 improves upto 100% identification for both the normal and the trauma statesfor the given facial features. The Figs. 6.21 and 6.22 depict the perfect matching between Target vs. Output plot to show that the network performs well for epochs 1000 compared to the case of epochs being 100.

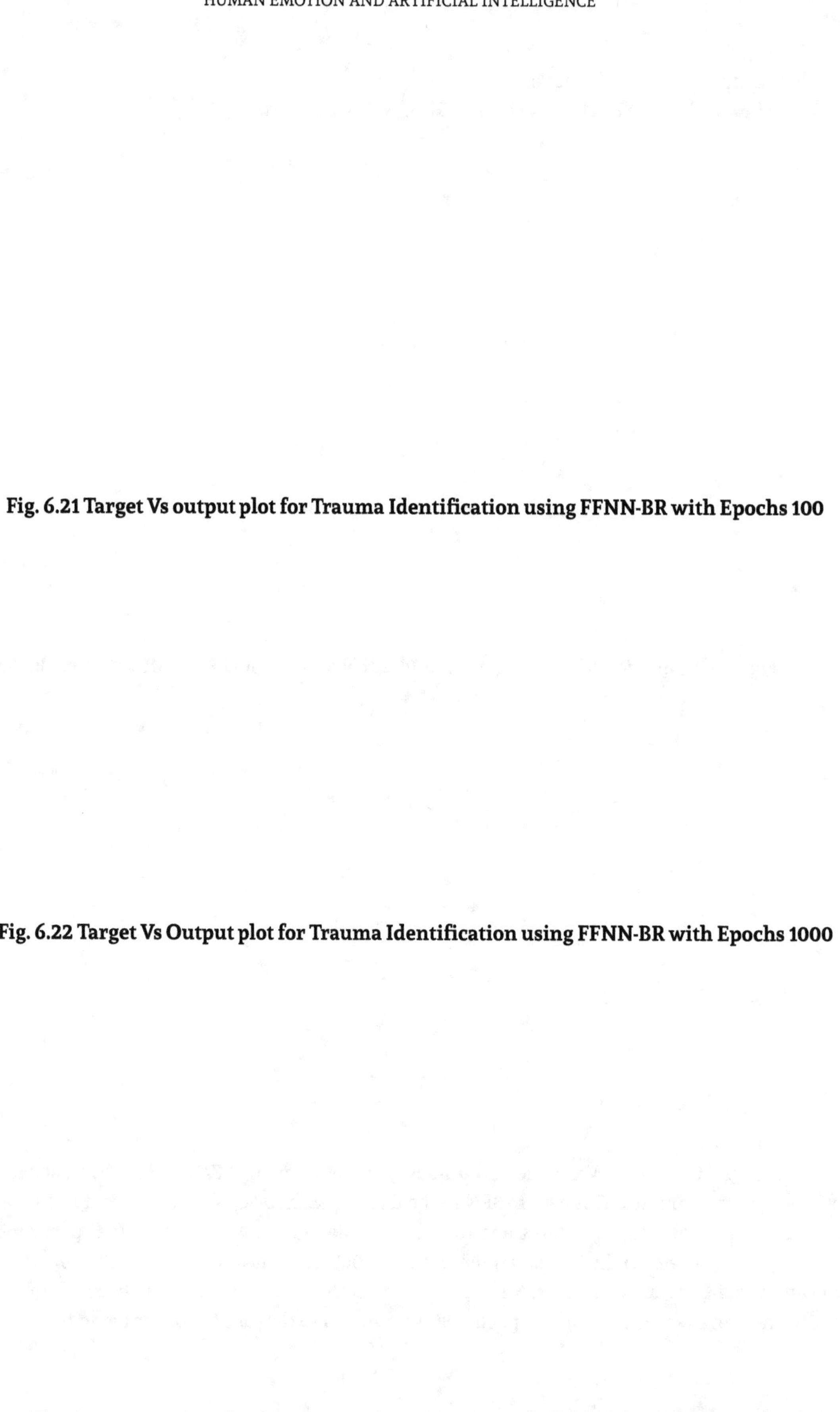

Fig. 6.21 Target Vs output plot for Trauma Identification using FFNN-BR with Epochs 100

Fig. 6.22 Target Vs Output plot for Trauma Identification using FFNN-BR with Epochs 1000

Fig. 6.23 Regression Plot for Trauma Identification using FFNN-BR with Epochs 100

Fig. 6.24 Regression Plot for Trauma Identification using FFNN-BR with Epochs 1000

The output equation derived using RNN-BPN reads as to be 0.33*Target+1e-16as seen in the Fig. 6.23 and on assumption of the target as 0.1, the output becomes 0.033 to indicate that with 100 epochs the network does not work efficiently, and so alsofor the R value equal to 0.5477, it indicates the poor system prediction capability.The output equation with 1000 epochs follows to be equal to 1*Target+1.4e-16as observed from the Fig. 6.24 and becomes equal to 0.1 for the same target of 0.1 and hence precisely indicates the trauma condition.

The plot in the Fig. 6.26 for the epochs 1000 indicates the error range of 0 to 1 and the networks poor prediction capability.The plot in the Fig. 6.26for the epochs 1000 indicates the zero error; while the histogram in the Fig. 6.27for the epochs 100 shows the maximum error to lie in the zero range but some of the error go out of the zero range to indicate the misclassification in identification of the emotions.

The Fig.6.28 exhibits the histogram analysis for the epochs 1000, where the maximum errors lie in the zero range and none occur outside to provide a perfect identification of the state of emotion. The summary of the performance obtained using RNN-BPN seen in the Table.6.3for both 100 and 1000 epochshighlight the outcome of the study.

Fig. 6.25 Error Plot for Trauma Identification using FFNN-BR with Epochs 100

Fig. 6.26 Error plot for Trauma Identification using FFNN-BR with Epochs 1000

Fig. 6.27 Error Histogram for Trauma Identification using FFNN-BR with Epochs 100

Fig. 6.28 Error Histogram for Trauma Identification using FFNN-BR with Epochs 1000

Table 6.3 Performance Evaluation of RNN with BPN Algorithm with the Epochs 100 and 1000.

Parameters

Epochs

100

Epochs

1000

Description

Error

0.0952

0

Incorrect Identification for epochs 100. Ideal value is zero has been achieved for epochs 1000

Accuracy

0.9048

1

Closeness of identification to original expression of a class Ideal value is 1 has been achieved for epochs 100 but it is an unfair value because of poor sensitivity value, and the ideal value of 1 has been achieved for epochs 1000 and it is considered as the fair value because both sensitivity and specificity are high.

Precision

1

1

Closeness of identification to original expression of a class and identification of expression not belonging to the same class. Ideal value is 1 and it has achieved for epochs 1000

Specificity

1

1

Correct identification of objects not belonging to a class Ideal value is 1.

Sensitivity

0.333

1

Correct identification of objects belonging to a class Ideal value is 1.

6.7 PERFORMANCE EVALUATION OF RNN WITH BR ALGORITHM

• 84 •

Fig. 6.29 Confusion Matrix for Trauma Identification using FFNN-BR with Epochs 100

Fig. 6.30 Confusion Matrix for Trauma Identification using FFNN-BR with Epochs 1000

Fig. 6.31 Target Vs Output plot for Trauma Identification using FFNN-BR with Epochs 100

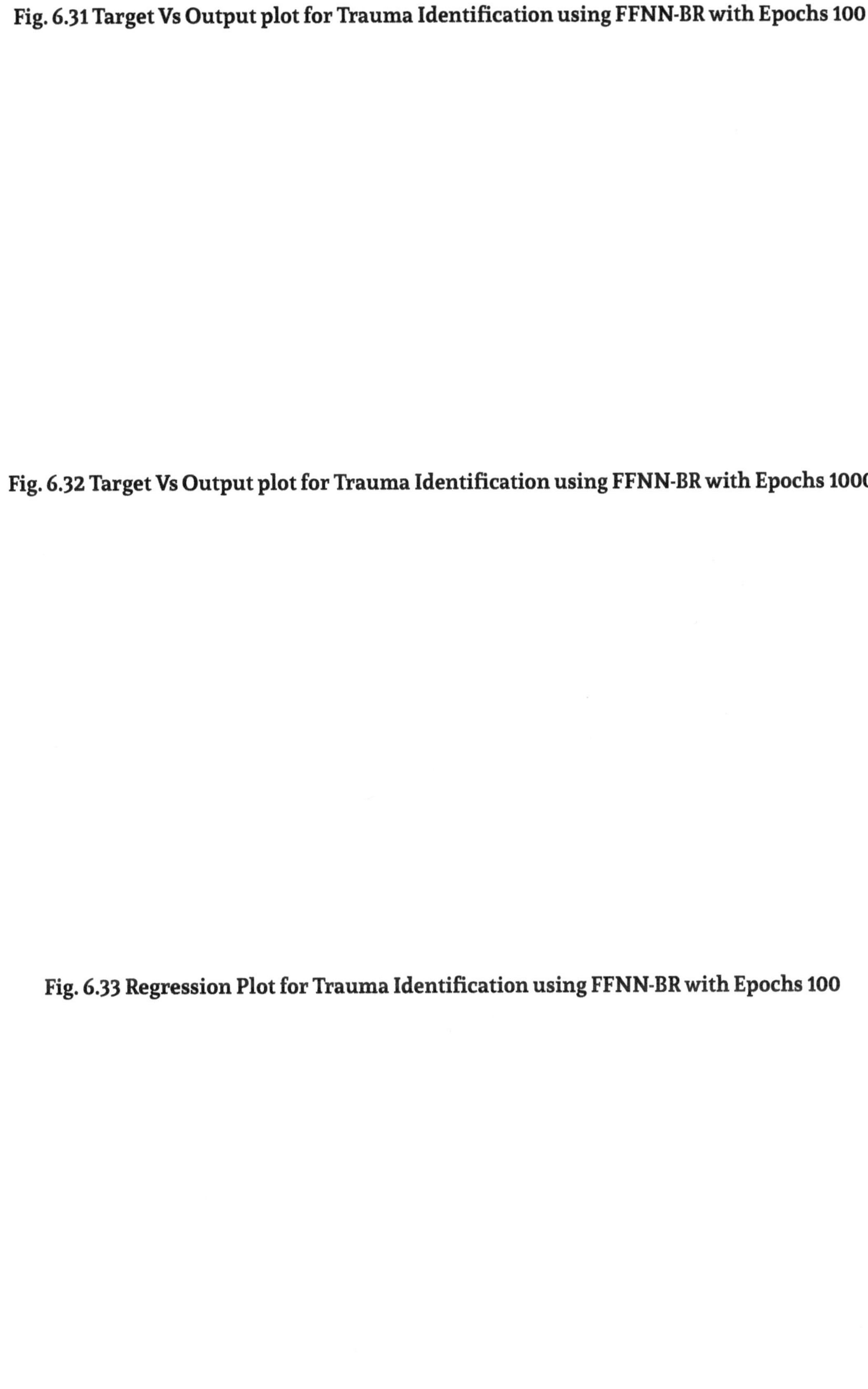

Fig. 6.32 Target Vs Output plot for Trauma Identification using FFNN-BR with Epochs 1000

Fig. 6.33 Regression Plot for Trauma Identification using FFNN-BR with Epochs 100

Fig. 6.34 Regression Plot for Trauma Identification using FFNN-BR with Epochs 1000

The confusion matrices in Figs.6.29 and 6.30 respectively relate to both in the lower (epochs 100)and the higher end (epochs 1000) show that the performance of the network remains the same in order that it identifies the normal emotion of the person upto 98.1 % and the trauma upto 33.3%.

The plots in the Figs. 6.31 and 6.32 bring out the imperfect fit between the target and the output for both the epochs 100 and 1000 to indicate the misidentification of the emotions.

The Figs. 6.33 and 6.34show that the equation travels asOutput=0.31*Target+0.019 for both the epochs 100 and 1000 and with a target assumed as 1 and the regression value as 0.45177, the output becomes equal to =0.31*1+0.019=0.401 which does not confirm with the desired output.

Fig. 6.35 Error Plot for Trauma Identification using FFNN-BR with Epochs 100

Fig. 6.36 Error Plot for Trauma Identification using FFNN-BR with Epochs 1000

Fig. 6.37 Error Histogram for Trauma Identification using FFNN-BR with Epochs 100

Fig. 6.38 Error Histogram for Trauma Identification using FFNN-BR with Epochs 1000

The error plot exhibits a horizontal line to reveal the zero error in the Figs. 6.35 and 6.36 in the span of -1 to +1. However from the histograms in the Figs. 6.37 and 6.38 it follows that the maximum error falls around the line of the zero error and only some of the bins fall beyond the zero range which indicates that the network almost perfectly identifies the state of the emotion and the trauma.

The Table 6.4 includes the details of the performance obtained through RNN with BR for both the epochs and speaks for the veracity to facilitate the choice of the algorithm.

Table 6.4 Performance Evaluation of RNN with BR Algorithm with the Epochs 100 and 1000.

Parameters	Epochs 100	Epochs 1000	Description
Error	0.11	0.11	Incorrect Identification. Ideal value is zero
Accuracy	0.89	0.89	Even though the accuracy is nearly equal to the ideal value of 1, but it is considered as the unfair value because of poor sensitivity value.
Precision	0.75	0.75	Closeness of identification to original expression of a class and identification of expression not belonging to the same class. Ideal value is 1.
Specificity	0.9815	0.9815	

The network almost can Correctly identify the objects not belonging to a class where the Ideal value is 1.

Sensitivity

0.333

0.333

The network poorer in Correct identification of objects belonging to a class Ideal value is 1.

Table 6.5 shows that RNN with BP algorithm with 1000 epochs works better in identifying the trauma condition of the person, which is very much able to differentiate between the normal state and trauma state of the person. But if we see in Table 4.5 we can note that emotion identification has been greatly identified using the RNN with BR algorithm with 1000 epochs and here we can conclude that RNN with BP algorithm is also working efficiently for this methodology at the stage of differentiation between the trauma and normal. And we can also see that both at table 4.5 and 6.5 the BPN and BRBPN algorithm prove to be best at their respective stages of classification at the higher end (i.e., for epochs 1000).

6.8 SUMMARY

The performance of FFNN and RNNhas been tested by BPN and BR and RNN with BPN algorithmswith two different cases of the epochs for the very basic emotions that include happy, neutral, and fear[Takeo Fujiwara(2015), GiotaStratou(2014), Caroline J. Bell(2017)] and anger being considered for identifying the trauma recognizing it to be hyper-reactive comparing with the reactions of thetrauma patients [Michael(2017)], [Carrie(2007)].It has been seen that it works well only with the good quality image and rejects the other images [Chaudary(2011)]. Besides it has been found that there exists difficulty in recognizing the traumatic situation in the case of fear and sadness because most of the trauma patients reveal these two expressions very often.

SEVEN

PERFORMANCE EVALUATION OF ANFIS FOR TRAUMAIDENTIFICATIONUSING THE CONCEPT OF ANOVA

7.1 INTRODUCTION

The state of trauma continues to be a contentious issue and inevitably causes a concern in the sense it disrupts the routine life of an individual. The increasing cases of trauma in recent times owing to a number of reasons become even more serious and can further hamper the life. It invites measures to quickly recognize the state and serve as a diagnostic platform where remedies can be initiated.

The fundamental structure of the FFNN andRNN form a base for designing the neural networks and enable conceiving different types of working model where FFNN can allow the data to travel one way only from input to output. The RNN networks on the other hand can see the passage of the signals travelling in both directions by introducing loops in the networks. Although both offer to detect the emotions and identify the trauma still the results remain rare from being satisfactory.

The ANFIS forms a hybrid system-incorporating the learning abilities of the ANN and excellent knowledge representation together with the inference capabilities of fuzzy logic that enjoy the ability to self modify their membership function for achieving a desired performance.

The studies in the literature from Premanand et al., (2016) use Local Directional Number Pattern(LDNP) for extracting the features and operate using use both SVM and FFNN. It follows that while the SVM performance remains in the average scale, the FFNN shows the increase in accuracy. The works of Shamla Mantri, Kalpana Bapat (2011) relate the efficiency of achieving the face recognition by neural network (NN) and the studies of Belal Ahmad et al (2016) use the NN approach based on face recognition, feature extraction and categorization to analyze the emotion.

Problem Definition

The effort engages to identify trauma with the help of the ANFIS on the MATLAB platform. Owing to the inert fact that ANFISrequires a larger number of rules for the specified number of twenty fourinputs, it becomes necessary to reduce the number of inputs to four by the concept of ANOVA. The investigation augurs the use of the FFNN and RNNand arriving at identifying the traumatic state with the reduced number of inputs and evaluate the performance through the same metrics.

Proposed Methodology

The philosophy orients to evolve a scheme for identifying trauma from the normal human emotion and assuages to allow the neural network to work on the principles of ANFIS. The strategy explained in the Fig.7.1 involves the use of the back-propagation algorithmand test the performance for the same 100 and 1000 epochs.

The exercise finds that while giving 100 epochs,an early stopping occurs and the ANFIS stops training at 3 epochs to avoid overfitting problem, for the reduced number of inputs obtained using ANOVA. The steps detailed below underline the sequence of events in the implementation of the procedure in the MATLAB podium. The Fig. 7.3 relates to the threshold setting for ANFIS in the event of the identification of the trauma image for the chosen values of the targets.

Step 1: When giving 24 inputs for ANFIS, the Matlab runs out of memory because of creation of a large number of rules
Step 2: It introduces the concept of ANOVA
Step 3: Number of inputs reduces from 24 to 4 inputs as shown in Fig. 7.2.
Step4: It sets a threshold of 0 for the efficient differentiation of trauma from normal human emotion as shown in Fig. 7.3
Step5: When the target = 0 and
Output is equal to 0 (ANFIS considers as the normal person)
When the target=1 and
Output is equal to 1 (ANFIS considers the person to be affected by trauma)

Fig 7.2 Parameters chosen after the implementation of ANOVA for trauma identification

Fig 7.3Matlab given Target value and based on that the Threshold setting for ANFIS

7.2Performance Evaluation of Adaptive Neuro Fuzzy Inference System with Backpropagation Algorithm using the concept of ANOVA

The histogram plot depicts the dispersion of the system errors as a measure of anomalies, where the anomalies reflect the data points which fit between the original and the target class significantly worse than the majority of the data.

The confusion matrix relates to be an error matrix portrayed by a table layout which helps in bringing out the performance of classifier. The columns of the confusion matrix represent the instances in the output class whereas the rows represent the instances in the actual class.

The Fig. 7.4 shows the confusion matrix with the diagonal elements being one and the off-diagonal elements to be 0 expressing the exact identification of the expression of the emotion by ANFIS.

Fig. 7.4 Confusion Matrixfor Trauma Identification with ANFIS

Fig. 7.5 Error Plotfor Trauma Identification with ANFIS

The horizontal line obtained using ANFIS in Fig.7.5 indicates a zero error for all the inputs.The plot drawn between the system outputs and the actual classes in Fig.7.6 for the regression value of 1 exhibit a perfect fit because in ANFIS system the values of the regression plot for training, validation and testing for entire the data set remain equal to 1.

Fig. 7.6 Regression Plotfor Trauma Identification with ANFIS

Fig. 7.7 Target Vs output plotfor Trauma Identification with ANFIS

The target pronounces the correct or decided value for the response associated with the specified the input. Usually the comparison between the output and the input serves to guide the learning process necessitating changes in the weight.

The perfect matching between the target plot and the output plot in the Fig. 7.7 shows the network works efficiently as a good classifier. The readings in the Table.7.1 bring out the merits of the ANFIS in being able to ideally identify the state of trauma from the emotions.

It can be seen from the Fig.7.8 that the maximum errors fall between -0.1 and-0.05 in the sense the error for entire input fall within this span which indicates that the approach recognizes correctly the expressions.

Fig.7. Error Histogram for Trauma Identification with ANFIS

Table 7.1: Performance Evaluation for Trauma Identification with ANFIS

NeuralNetwork

ANFIS- Trauma

Accuracy

1

Precision

1

Sensitivity

1

Specificity

1
MAE
0

In this table all the parameters shows the ideal value which indicates the best identification of ANFIS between the emotion and Trauma state

7.3 Performance Evaluation of Trauma Identification with FFNN-BPN using the conceptof ANOVA

Fig. 7.9 Confusion Matrixfor Trauma Identification using FFNN-BPN-ANOVA with 8 epochs

Fig. 7.10 Error Plotfor Trauma Identification using FFNN-BPN-ANOVA with 8 epochs

The confusion matrix in the Fig. 7.9shows that the FFNN-BPN with ANOVA identifies the normal condition of the person correctly upto 98.1% and that of thetraumaonly upto 22.2%. The plot in the Fig. 7.10,with the span of -1 to 1, on not being able to extract a horizontal line at zero error display the poor predication capability.

The FFN-BPN gives the regression value as 0.3347 which falls far away from the ideal value of 1 as seen from the Fig 7.11. The output equation for the regression plot reads as Output=0.2*Target+0.019 and calculates to be as 0.2*1+0.019=0.219, for a target of 1, which again does not relate to the desired output value.

Fig. 7.11 Regression Plotfor Trauma Identification using FFNN-BPN-ANOVA with 8 epochs

Fig. 7.12 Target Vs Output Plot for Trauma Identification using FFNN-BPN-ANOVA with 8 epochs

The target being the correct value for the response associated with the chosen input allows the NN to be guided with the choice of weights in the learning process. The output plot in the Fig. 7.12 deviates away explaining its inability to differentiate between the normal and trauma condition. The error histogram in the Fig 7.13 shows nearly 60% of value lies near the zero range, but still there exists errors beyond the zero range to reflect the error in the classification. The indices in the Table. 7.2 summarize the performance of the FFNN-BPN with ANOVA for 8 epochs in its efforts to identify trauma.

7.13 Error Histogramfor Trauma Identification using FFNN-BPN-ANOVA with 8 epochs

Table 7.2: Performance evaluation of FFNN-BPN with ANOVA for 8 epochs for Trauma Identification

Parameters

Epochs

8

Description

Specificity

0.98

The network shows almost correct identification of the objects not belonging to a class and the ideal value is 1.

Sensitivity

0.22

The network shows the poor identification of objects belonging to a class.

Accuracy

0.87

It is considered as an unfair value because of lower sensitivity value. As explained in table 4.1.

Precision

0.66

The precision value doesnot reveal an improved network performance in identification

MAE

0.13

Incorrect identification and the ideal value is zero

7.4 Trauma Identification using FFNN-BR with the concept of ANOVA

The FFNN-BR offers the same output for both the upper and the lower endin view of the fact that it doesnot bring out any improvement in performance on an increase in the number of epochs from 100 to 1000. The Fig. 7.14construes to conclude the abnormal behavior with the FFNN-BR algorithm, irrespective of the nature of the expression to which the network remains subjected and the number of epochs.

The error plot of horizontal line in the Fig. 7.15indicates the zero error with the span of 0 to 1 to explain the misclassification of the expressions

Fig. 7.14 Confusion Matrixfor Trauma Identification using FFNN-BR-ANOVA for both 100 and 1000 Epochs

Fig. 7.15 Error Plotfor Trauma Identification using FFNN-BR-ANOVA for both 100 and 1000 Epochs

Fig. 7.16 Regression Plotfor Trauma Identification using FFNN-BR-ANOVA for both 100 and 1000 Epochs

Fig. 7.17 Target Vs Output Plotfor Trauma Identification using FFNN-BR-ANOVA for both 100 and 1000 Epochs

The regression value of zero in the Fig.7.16 exhibits that the network through the use of the ANOVA with the FFNN-BRdoes not succeed in distinguishing between the normal and trauma caseto explain the in suitability of the model under study.However the mismatch between the target and the output plot in the Fig. 7.17reveals the inefficiency in identifying the emotions

Fig. 7.18 Error Plotfor Trauma Identification using FFNN-BR-ANOVA for both 100 and 1000 Epochs

The error histogram inthe Fig. 7.18shows that nearly 50% of the data falls near the zero line and the remaining to exist beyond the zero line which argues to be the reason for some of the expressions to be identified wrongly. The entries in the Table.7.3 describe the performance of the network for the different parameters and the chosen two epochs.

Table 7.3: Performance evaluation for Trauma identification by using FFNN-BR with ANOVA for both 100 and 1000 epochs

Parameters

Epochs

100 and 1000

Description

Specificity

1

Shows the ideal value of 1.

Sensitivity

0

The system doesnot show any sensitivity

Accuracy

0.85

The accuracy is considered as an unfair value because the value of accuracy is highly based on specificity. The accuracy may be considered as the fair value only when both sensitivity and specificity are high or low.

Precision

0

The system doesnot show any precision.

MAE

0.142

Incorrect identification and the ideal value is zero

7.5 Trauma identification with RNN-BPN using ANOVA

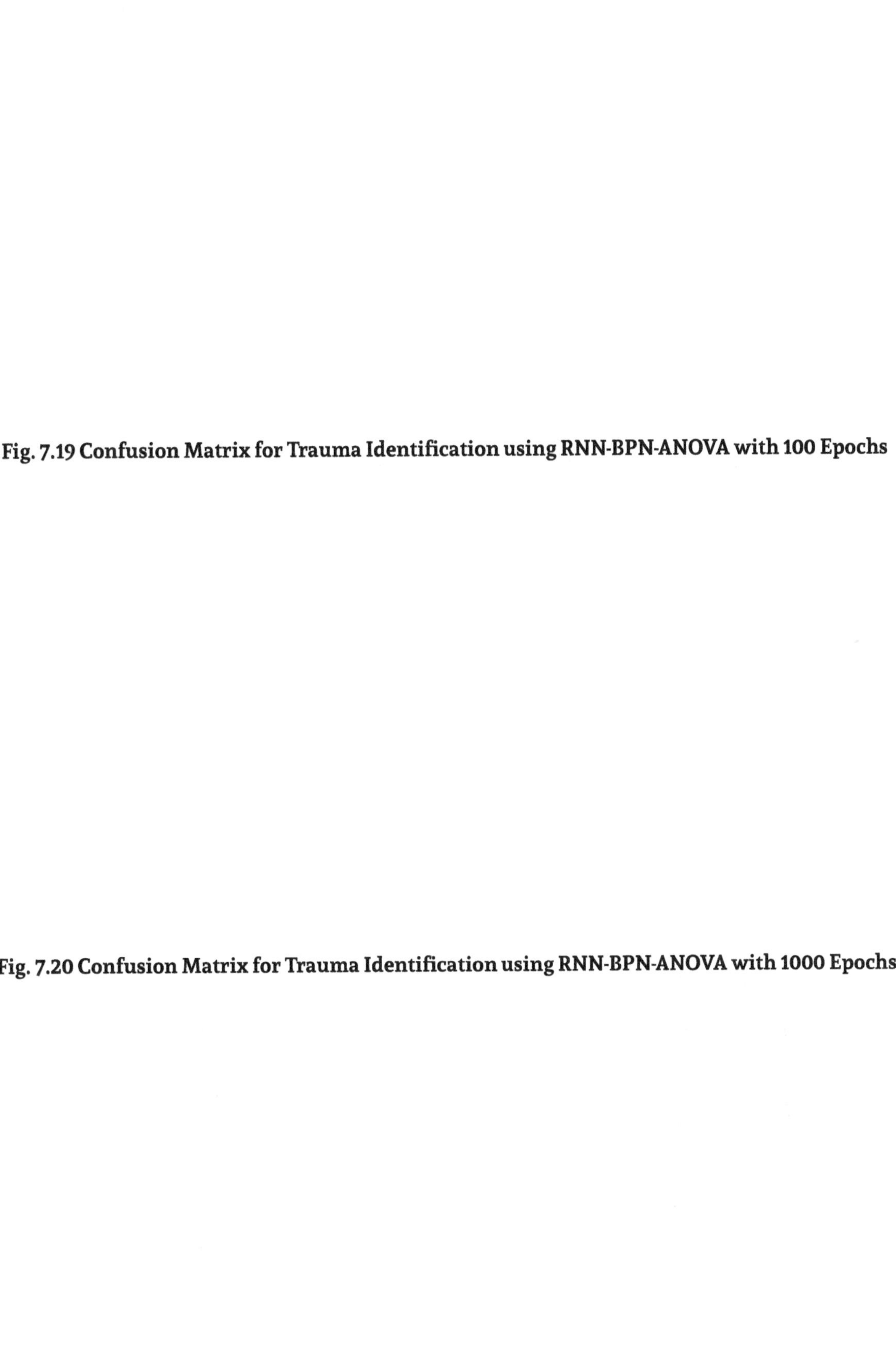

Fig. 7.19 Confusion Matrix for Trauma Identification using RNN-BPN-ANOVA with 100 Epochs

Fig. 7.20 Confusion Matrix for Trauma Identification using RNN-BPN-ANOVA with 1000 Epochs

Fig. 7.21 Error Plot for Trauma Identification using RNN-BPN-ANOVA with 100 Epochs

Fig. 7.22 Error plot for Trauma Identification using RNN-BPN-ANOVA with 1000 Epochs

The confusion matrix for the epochs 100 in the Fig. 7.19 through ANOVA with the RNN-BPN identifies the normal condition of the person upto 98.1% and the network does not react to the trauma condition. However on increasing the number of epochs to 1000,the network serves to identify the normal condition of the person upto 98.1 and that of trauma correctly upto 55.6% as seen from the Fig. 7.20.

The horizontal line in the error Plot shown in the Figs. 7.21 and 7.22indicate the zero error over a span from -1 to +1 for both the cases. The regression value of 0.051848 shows the poor classification for epochs 100 as observed from the Fig. 7.23and that of 0.62419for epochs 1000in the Fig. 7.24explains the completeness of the model across the range from 0 to 1.

Fig. 7.23 Regression Plot for Trauma Identification using RNN-BPN-ANOVA with 100 Epochs

Fig. 7.24 Regression plot for Trauma Identification using RNN-BPN-ANOVA with 1000 Epochs

Fig. 7.25 Target Vs output plot for Trauma Identification using RNN-BPN-ANOVA with 100 Epochs

Fig. 7.26 Target Vs output plot for Trauma Identification using RNN-BPN-ANOVA with 1000 Epochs

Fig. 7.27 Error Histogram for Trauma Identification using RNN-BPN-ANOVA with 100 Epochs

Fig. 7.28 Error Histogram for Trauma Identification using RNN-BPN-ANOVA with 1000 Epochs

The imperfect matching between the target and the output plot in the Figs. 7.25 and 7.26 depicts the misclassification of emotionsfor both the epochs 100 and 1000.

The Figs 7.27 and 7.28 projects that while 50% of value lies near the zero range for epochs 100, 60% of the value lies near the zero range for epochs 1000 to enumerate the improvement in the process of classification on increasing the number of epochs.

The parametric indices in the Table.7.4 elucidate the summary of the performance of the network for the two different epochs to fructify the ability in terms of the identifying perception.

Table 7.4: Performance evaluation of RNN-BPN for 100 and 1000 epochs

Parameters	Epochs 100	Epochs 1000	Description
Specificity			

0.9815

1

The specificity exhibits the ideal value of 1 for 1000 epochs, but for 100 epochs it remains close to the ideal value.
Sensitivity

0

0.556

The network remains insensitive with 100 epochs and for 1000 epochs it shows improvement in sensitivity
Accuracy

0.841

0.93

The accuracy appears to be an unfair value because of the lower sensitivity even though it is near the ideal value of 1 for both 100 and 1000 epochs.

Precision

0

1

The network shows zero precision for epochs 100 and for 1000 epochs it shows the ideal value of 1
MAE

0.1587

0.063

Both 100 and 1000 epochs donot show the ideal value of 0 which indicates the error in identification.

7.6 Performance Evaluation of RNN-BR for Trauma Identification using the Concept of ANOVA

The network operating with the architecture of RNN-BR and ANOVA does not offer any improvement in performance in the sense it shows the same output for both the upper and the lower endon increasing the number of epochs.

However with the RNN-BR algorithm, the performance retrieves to be a little unexpected as seen from the confusion matrix in the Fig. 7.29irrespective of the expression to which the network remains subjected.

Fig. 7.29 Confusion Matrixfor Trauma Identification using RNN-BR-ANOVA for both 100 and 1000 Epochs

Fig. 7.30 Error Plotfor Trauma Identification using RNN-BR-ANOVA for both 100 and 1000 Epochs

Fig. 7.31 Regression Plotfor Trauma Identification using RNN-BR-ANOVA for both 100 and 1000 Epochs

Fig.7.32 Target Vs Output Plotfor Trauma Identification using RNN-BR-ANOVA for both 100 and 1000 Epochs

Fig. 7.33Error histogramfor Trauma Identification using RNN-BR-ANOVA for both 100 and 1000 Epochs

The nature of the error plot in the Fig. 7.30,with the span of 0 to 1 indicates the misclassification of expressions.The Fig 7.31 indicates that the network with the RNN-BR algorithm for the regression value of zero turns out to be unsuitable for differentiating between the trauma and normal human expression.

The Fig. 7.32 shows that the system doesnot exhibit a perfect matching between the target and output plot.It follows from the Fig. 7.33that nearly 50% of the data falls near the zero line and the remaining exist beyond the zero line to indicate the improper identification of some of the expressions. The Table.7.5 summarizes the performance of the network in terms of the parametric indices for the two chosen epochs. **Table 7.5 Performance evaluation of RNN-BR with ANOVA for Trauma identification for 100 and 1000 epochs**

Parameters

For epochs

100 and 1000

Description

Specificity

1

Shows the ideal value of 1.

Sensitivity

0

The correct identification of the objects belonging to a class reveals an ideal value of 1. But the value shows the network to remain insensitive.

Accuracy

0.67

The accuracy appears to be an unfair value because of the lower sensitivity even though it falls near the ideal value of 1 for both the epochs 100 and 1000.

Precision

0

It does not shows a number

MAE

0.14

The incorrect identification reveals the ideal value of zero

Table 7.6 Comparison of Performance between Normal Emotion and Trauma identification with ANFIS

S.

No.

Performance Evaluation

Trauma Detection

1.

No.of Inputs

4

2.

Algorithm

Backpropagation

3.

Membership Function

Trimf

4.

Transfer Function

Hyperbolic Tan Sigmoid

5.

Error Histogram

Nearly 100% of value lies near the zero line which indicates the perfect identification of the emotions and Trauma.

6.

Error Plot

Zero error

7.

Regression Plot

R=1(indicate the perfect fit)

8.

Confusion matrix

Trauma state has been identified correctly

9.

Specificity

1

10.

Sensitivity

1

11.

Accuracy

1

12.

Precision

1

13.

Mean Absolute Error

0

From the table 7.7, we can see that the concept of ANOVA does not work well in identifying the trauma state of the person from the normal emotion.

From the table 8.5 we conclude that the working of ANFIS with concept of ANOVA is good and with the concept of ANOVA the number of inputs is also reduced and the output for both emotion detection and trauma identification from normal emotion has been identified at the lower bound itself, so we can say ANFIS works better for the proposed work.

7.7 SUMMARY

The study has been intrigued to identify the normal and traumatic states of a person in the framework of the FFNN and RNNthrough BPN and BR algorithm with the concept of ANOVA, and also used ANFIS with the same concept of ANOVA. The performance has been evaluated through parametric indices that include Error histogram, Error Plot, Confusion Matrix, Mean Absolute Error, target Vs output plot, specificity, sensitivity, accuracy and precision. The exercise has been laid to follow the chosen ideal values for distinguishing between the correct and incorrect classifications. It has been elucidated that ANFIS with the concept of ANOVA works better at the lower end itself(i.e., epochs 3) in identifying the trauma compared to FFNNwith BPN and BR algorithm with epochs 100 and 1000 and RNN withBPN and BR algorithm with epochs 100 and 1000.

Usually trauma identification in hospital is done by framing a set of questions, which are directly or indirectly associated with symptoms of trauma, so that patient with higher score(goes beyond the threshold) is identified as trauma patients, but there may be possibility that the patient can answer the questions wrongly by misunderstanding or wantedly to avoid hospital environment or medicine, or they may undergo scan which can produce sideffects.This can be overcome by this method of identifying trauma by having only the facial images.

EIGHT

CHAPTER 8
CONCLUSION

8.1 GENERAL

The automatic facial expression recognition appears to be imperative for the natural human-machine interaction and find scope in a host of fieldsthat include behavioral and social science among others. Although the humans perceive the facial expressions immediately and effortlessly, the reliable automatic facial expression recognition by a machine still offers scope.

The process encompasses to correctly identifying the normal human emotions in the form of happy, sad, anger, neutral, disgust and fear besides being able to differentiate the normal emotion of the human from the traumatic state of the person.

The emphasis revolves around the use of hybrid methods for automatic facial expression recognition through the use of ANN related networks. The features extracted from the image undergo training after being quantified using FFNN, RNN and ANFIS..

8.2 CONTRIBUTIONS

The first exercise has been oriented to measure the dimensions of the images that include the area, orientation, perimeter, solidity, major axis length, minor axis length and centroid. It has been based on the extraction of the features from the chosen image and preprocessed to create the enhanced image from it obtains their orientation and size. The facial expression recognition (FER) has been obtained usingthe JAFFEdatabase with 180 images which consist of 6 different expressions.

The second major effort has been related to recognize the emotions through the use of the FFNN and RNN using both BPN and BRBPN with varying number of epochs. It has been observed that when using FFNN- BPN algorithmthe network undergoes early stopping with eight epochs itself. However when using FFNN with Bayesian Regularized Backpropagation (BRBPN)) algorithm and the RNN with both the BPN and the BRBPN, the algorithm has been run for both lower end (100 epochs)and higher end(1000 epochs) and the performance evaluated. The results in terms of metrics have been elicited to project that the RNN with BRBPN algorithm serves to correctly identify the emotion.

The next endeavor has been ordained to the introduction of ANFIS for identifying the emotions of the person. The ANFIS has been known to be based on the principles of the fuzzy logic. The fuzzy rules have been created based on the number of inputs and the membership function. The procedure has been sought to operate with the triangular membership function (trimf). However owing to the excess requirement of memory space, the methodology has been laid to invoke the use of ANOVA and thus allow a reduction in the number of inputs.

The performance of the ANFIS has been tested for the lower end with BPN algorithm and the results reveal that at 3 epochs itself the ANFIS extracts a closer recognition. The exercise has also been examined with FFNN and RNN with the use of both the BPN and BRBPN algorithm for both 100 and 1000 epochs along with the concept of ANOVA. In any case the results from the FFNN and RNN have not been observed to show an improvement in the performance.

The third effort has been oriented to the identification of the state of traumaof the person, being different from the normal emotion of the sadness. It has been articulated through the use of the PICS database and involves the trial and errorsetting of the threshold as 0.22 based on target value. The methodology has been laid in order that when the value lies within the threshold, the network identifies it as the normal emotions and when it goes beyond threshold the condition defines it to be as trauma.

Though the RNN with BPN algorithm has been found to show encouraging results, still when tried with both lower and higher epochs; it has been portrayed that the RNN with BPN and BRBPN algorithm and the FFNN with BRBPN algorithm have not been able to classify the emotions correctly. However it has been noticed that with the increase in the number of epochs, the performance has been increased enabling the network to provide good prediction capability when compared with the performance at the lower end.

The fourth endeavor has again been focused on the identification of the trauma and the metrics bring out a much better capability for the ANFIS over the FFNN and RNN. It has been elicited that the ANFIS offers to be the best suited for both expression recognition and differentiating the trauma from the normal human emotion at the lower end itself. The identification of trauma has been extended to a case where the trauma has been considered to be a psychological pain inside the patients.

8.3 Limitations of the study

The data under study consists of facial images taken from JAFFE database which include only the Japanese female image for normal human emotion.

The experiments operate in a restricted framework only with 2D black and white images.

8.4 Scope of the Future Work

- The exercise may be conducted on more diverse database and make the process of classification more useful.
- The procedure can be extended to identify 3D images either black and white or color images.
- The number of emotions can be increased and the study made more general. .

As given in section 2.2, among the two methods of identifying facial expression detection, we go by direct method of identifying human emotion and the Fig 2.1 showed the recent methods used for extracting facial features and their disadvantages and we have overcome the disadvantages of those direct methods and our methodology works with,

- High recognition rate of upto 99% has been achieved
- Computationally efficient and simple.
- Reduction in feature vector dimension and reduction in computational time.
- Work equally well for low resolution as well as for good quality / high resolution images
- Expression analysis and recognition done in more conducive manner
- Since we don't go with texture the proposed methodology works irrespective of rays
- The network works efficiently with lower epochs and less number of inputs (ANFIS).
- If we depend on Action Unit or Active Appearance Model the number of inputs given for the network will be varying depending on the image given or the number of inputs will be more for identifying the emotion, but here the higher recognition rate has been achieved for nearly 260 images with the standard input.
- Here with RNN-BR for epochs 1000(for classification of six different emotions), RNN-BPN for epochs 1000 (for identifying Trauma) and for ANFIS with epochs 3, no false assumption has been made by the network and the given 260 images has been classified correctly
- In the proposed work dimension for eyes, eyebrows and mouth are measured and trained by the neural network no need of considering the full face.

References

1. Aann Zane. M (2014), Analysis of Distance Measures for Human Eyebrow Recognition Using Fast Template Matching , International Journal of Emerging Technology and Advanced Engineering , Volume 4 Issue 2, April

2. Allaerts B, Mennesson J, Bilasco I M, Djeraba C (2017), Impact of face registration techniques on facial expression recognition, Signal Processing: Image Communication,Nov, pp 44-53,.

3. Anagha S. Dhavalikar, RK. Kulkami (2014),Face detection and facial expression recognition system,Proceedings of IEEE International Conference in Electronics and communication systems (ICECS), Feb.

4. Anas Abouyahya, Sanaa El Fkihi, Rachid Oulad Haj Thami, DrissAboutadine (2016), "Feature Extraction for Facial Expression Recognition", 5th IEEE International conference on Mltimedia computing and systems(ICMCS), 29 September-1 October.

5. Archana Rathi, Brijesh N Shah (2016), Facial Expression Recognition, International Research Journal of Engineering and Technology (IRJET), Volume 3, Issue 4, April.

6. Annett Schirmer, Ralph Adolphs (2017), Emotion Perception from Face, Voice and Touch: Comparisons and Convergence, Cell Press, Trends in Cognitive Science, Vol. 21, No.3, March.

7. Ayesha Butalia, Maya Ingle, Parakulkarni (2012), Facial expression recognition for security, International Journal of Modern engineering research(IJMER) Vol.2 , Issue 4, July-Aug.

8. Belal Ahmad, Ravinder Kumar, Marghoob Ahmad Usmani (2016), Facial Expression Recognition Using Artificial Neural Network, IJEDR1603108 International Journal of Engineering Development and Research (IJEDR), Volume 4, Issue 3, August.

9. Boughrara H (2014).,"Facial expression Recognition based on a MLP neural network using constructive training algorithm", Journal of Multimedia Tools and Applications(Springer), 28th October.

10. Caroline J. Bell (2017), Earthquake brain: Altered Recognition and Misclassification of facial expression are related to trauma exposure but not posttraumatic stress disorder, Frontiers in psychiatry, Volume 8, December.

11. Carrie L Masten, Amanda E Guyer, Hilary Hodgdon and Erin B tone (2008)., Recognition of facial emotions among maltreated children with high rates of post-traumatic stress disorder, Published by internation congress on Child Abuse and Neglect; International Society for the Prevent of Child Abuse and Neglect,Elsevier, Article 32(1): 1399-53, February

12. Caifeng Shag, Shaogang Gong, and *McOwan*W. Peter (2009), Facial Expression recognition based on Local Binary Patterns: A comprehensive study,*Image and vision Computing, Volume 27, Issue 6*, pp 803-816, May.

13. Chaudary Muhammad Aqdus, Mohammad Ahsanul Haque, Matthias rehm and Kamal Nasrollahi (2018), Facial Expression Recognition for Traumatic Brain Injured Patients, September, Proceedings of the 13th International conference on Computer Vision, Imaging and Computer Graphics Theory and Applications, Volume 4, pages 522-530, January.

14. ChristofferHolmgard, Georgios N. Yannaakis, Karen Inge Karstoft, Henrik Steen Andersen(2013), Stress detection for PTSD Via the Startle Mart Game, Human Association IEEE Conference on Affective Computing and Intelligent Interaction, 12 December.

15. Christopher K. GermerAnd Kristin Neff, Cultivating self-compassion in Trauma Survivors, Follette_Book.indb, pp 43-56, May,2014

16. Chi, Lianhua Chi, Meng Fang, JueboWu (2015), Facial Expression Recognition Based on cloud Model, International Archives of the Photogrammetry, Remote Sensing and Spatial Information Sciences,Vol.387, PartII, February.

17. Chih-chin Lai, Chung-Hung ko (2014), Facial expression recognition based on two stage features extraction", Article in optik-International Journal of LightElectorn Optics 125(22):6678-6680, November.

18. Daniel Acevedo, Pablo Negri, Maria Elena Buemi, Francisco Gomez Fernandez and Marta Mejail (2017), "A simple geometric-based descriptor for Facial expression recognition", 12[th]IEEE International conference on Automatic Face and Gesture Recognition, May 30-June 2017.

19. Darwin C,(Originally Published in 1872, The Expression of Emotions in Man and Animals, Publisher: John Murray Online Edition: http://humannature.com/darwin/emotion/contents.html

20. Devi Arumugam, Dr. S. Purushothaman (2011), Emotion Classification Using Facial expression, International Journal of Advanced Computer Science and Application, Vol. 2, No. 7, April.

21. Deepthi.S ,Archana.G.S, Dr.JagathyRaj.V (2013), "Facial Expression Recognition Using Artificial Neural Networks"IOSR Journal of Computer Engineering (IOSRJCE) ISSN: 2278-0661, ISBN: 2278-8727, Volume 8, Issue 4 (Jan. - Feb.).

22. Debasmitachakrabarti, Debtanu Dutta (2013), "Facial expression Recognition Usign Eigenspaces, Procedia Technology(Elsevier), volume 10,Page 755-761, December.

23. Deepa .A, Sasipraba T.(2015), "Age estimation in facial images using angular classification technique", Advances in natural and applied sciences, Vol. 9, No.6,, September.

24. DebishreeDagar, AbirHudait, H.K. Tripathy, M.N. Das(2016), "Automatic Emotion Detection Model from facial Expression", International Conference on Advanced Communication Control and Computing Technologies(ICACCCT), May 25-27.

25. Dhrubajoti Boruah, Kandarpa Kumar sarma, Anjan Kumar Talukdar (2015), "Different face Regions detection based Facial Expression recognition", 2nd International Conference on Signal Procession and Integrated Network (SPIN),19-20 February.

26. Dileep M R, AjitDanti (2016), Human Emotion Classification based on Eyes and Mouth using Susan Edges, International Journal of Scientific and Engineering Research, Volume 7, Issue 7, July.

27. Edward Balke, Trauma and Conflict, Development DESTIN Studies Institute, Working Paper Seires,(LSE),ISSN 1470-2320, pp. 2-37,October 2002.

28. Ekman P (1973), "Darwin and facial expression; a century of research in review, edited by Paul Ekman", New York, Academic Press.

29. Ekman P and W.V. Friesen (1976), "Pictures of Facial Affect", Consulting Psychologists Press, Palo Alto.

30. Ekman P. And Friesen W (1978), Facial Action Coding System,Consulting, psychologists Press.

31. Fan Zhang, Kui Zhang, Yang Ji, Ning Liu (2009), Post-Trauma Mobile Service: A case Study of psychological Counseling Service with Mobile Internet Technology, IEEE International conference on New trends in Information and Service Science(NISS'09), August.

32. GengtaoZhow, Yongzho Zhan, Jianming Zhang (2006), Facial Expression Recognition Based on Selective Feature Extraction", Proceedings of the 6^{th}IEEE International Conference on Intelligent System Design and Applications(ISDA'06), date of conference 16-18 Oct 2006, date added to IEEE xplore 11 December 2006.

33. Ghimire D., Jeong S., Lee J., SunghwanJeong, Joonwhoan Lee, and San Hyun park(2017)., Facial expression recognition based on local region specific features and support vector machine,*Multimedia Tools and Applications*, Volume 76, Issure 6, pp 7803-7821, March.

34. Gheorghe Gile, NicegeorgeBizdoc (2015),Detecting human emotions with an adaptive Neuro fuzzy inference system", 6th International conference on computational Mechanics and virtual engineering comec-,15-16 oct-2015.

35. GiotaStratou, Stefan Schere, Jonathan Gratch, Louis-Philippe Morecy(2015), Automatic Non-Verbal Behavior Indicators of Depression and PTSD: Effect of gender,Volume 9, Issue 1, pp 17-29,March.

36. Gomathi V., Ramar K. and SanthiyakuJeevakumarA (2010), "A Neuro Fuzzy approach for facial expression recognition using LBP Histograms", International Journal of Computer theory and Engineering, Vol. 2, No.2, pp 245-249, April.

37. HayderAnkishan and Derya Yilmaz (2013) ,Comparison of SVM and ANFIS for snore related sounds classification using the largest lyapunovexponent and entropy, Hindawi publishing corporation Computational and mathematical Methods in Medicine, Article ID 23937, 13 pages, October.

38. HadiSeyedarabi, Ali Aghagolzadeh, SoharbKhanmihammadi (2004), "Recognition of six basic facial expression by feature-points tracking using RBF neural network and fuzzy inference system", Proceeding of IEEE International Conference on Multimedia and Expo(ICME), pp 1219-1222, Jan.

39. Happy S.L. and Routray A (2015)., "AutoamaticFacial Expression Recognition Using features of salient facial

patches," *IEEE Transactions on Affective Computing*,Vol.6, no.11, pp. 1-1, Jan-March

40. Hung-Fu huang and Shen-Chuan Tai (2012), Facial Expression Recognition Using New Feature Extraction Algorithm, Electronic Letters on Computer Vision and Image Analysis 11(1):41-54, 2012

41. Javaid Q., Arif M., Awan D., ShahaM.A (2016)., "Efficient facial expression detection by using the adaptive Neuro fuzzy inference system and the Bezier curve", Sindh university research journal(science series), vol.48(3), pp. 595-600, June.

42. Jun Ou, Xiao-Bo Bai, Yun Pei, Liang Ma, Wei Liu (2010), Automatic facial expression recognition using gabor filter and expression analysis, Proceedings on 2nd IEEE International Conference on Computer Modeling and Simulation, , pp 215-218, 22-24 January.

43. Jessie R. Balbin, Jasmine Nadja J.Pinugu, Abigail Joy S. Basco, Myla B. Cabanada, Patrish Melrose V. Gonzales, uan Carlos C. marasigan, Marianne M. Sejera (2017)., Development of Scientific System for Assessment of Post-traumatic Stress Disorder Patients using Physiological Sensors and Feature Extraction for Emotional State Analysis, 2017 IEEE 9th International conference on Humanoid, Nanotechnology, Informationo Technology, Communication and Control, Environment and management(HNICEM), date of Conference: 1-3 Jan, Added to IEEE Xplore 25 Jan 2018.

44. Junhua Li, Li Peng, "Feature Difference Matrix and QNNs for Facial Expression Recognition", 2008 Chinese Control and Decision Conference (CCDC 2008), pp. 3445-3449, date of conference 2-4 July 2008, date added to the IEEE Xplore 12 August 2008,

45. Kavitha, Varghese Paul and N.M. Jothi swaroopan (2017), "Biometric Emotion Recognition using Adaptive Nero fuzzy inference system", Middle east journal of scientific research 25(8): 1644-1649, 2017.

46. Kherchaoui S., HouacineA (2014), Facial Expression Identification System with Euclidean Distance of Facial Edges, International Conference of Soft Computing and pattern Recognition, 2014 6th international conference of soft computing and pattern Recognition(SoCPaR), date of conference 11-14 Aug 2014, date added to the IEEE Xplore: 15 Jan 2015.

47. KhoodijahHulliyah, Normi Sham Awang Abu Bakar, Amelia Ritahani Ismail (2016), "Emotion Recognition and Brain Mapping for Sentiment Analysis: A Review", 2017 Second International conference on iNformatics and computing(ICIC), pp. 2543-2546, date of Conference 1-3 November 2017, Date Added to IEEE Xplore 05 February 2018.

48. Khandait S.P., Thool R.C., Khandait P.D(2012a),Comparative Analysis of ANFIS and NEURAL approach for expression Recognition using Geometry Method, International Journal of Advanced Research in computer science and software Engineering, Vol. 2, Issue 3 March.

49. Khandait S.P., Thool R.C., Khandait P.D (2012b)., ANFIS and NN Based facial Expression Recognition using curvelet features, International Journal of computing, ISSN: 1727-6209, Vol-11, Issue 3, 255-261, December.

50. Khandait S.P., Thool R.C., KhandaitP.D.(2011),"Automatic Facial Feature Extraction and Expression Recognition based on Neural Network", (IJACSA), International Jounal of Advanced Computer Science and Applications, Vol. 2, No.1 January.

51. Khandait S.P., Thool R.C., Khandait P.D (2013), "ANFIS and BPNN based expression recognition using HFGA for feature extraction", Bulletin of Electrical Engineering and information, Vol.2, No.1, pp:11-22, March.

52. Kiran Talele, Archana ShirsatTejalUplenchwar, Kushal Tuckley (2016), "Facial Expression Recognition Using General Regression Neural Network", 2016 IEEE Bombay Section Symposium(IBSS), date of conference 21-22 Dec-2016, date added to IEEE Xplore 8th June 2017.

53. Kotsiaand Pitas I.(2007), Facial Expression Recognition in Image Sequences Using Geometric Deformation Features and Support Vector Machines. IEEE Transactions on Image Processing, Vol. 16, no. 1, pp. 172-187, Jan.

54. Kunika Verma, Ajay Khunteta(2010), "Facial Expression Recognition using Gabor Filter and Multi-layer Artificial Neural Network", IEEE international Conference on Information, Communication, Instrumentation and Control(ICICIC-2010), paper Id-347.

55. Latifa Greeche, MahaJazouli, Najia Es- Sbai, AichaMajda, ArsalaneZarghili (2017), Comparison Between Euclidean and Manhattan distance Measure for Facial Expressions Classification, 2017 International Conference on Wireless

Technologies, Embedded and Intelligent Systems(WITS),date Added to Conference 19-20 April 2017, Date added to IEEE Xplore 29 May 2017.

56. Lajevardi S.M. and Hussain Z.M (2009), Local feature extraction methods for facial expression recognition, in the proceeding of 17th European signal Processing Conference (EUSIPCO), date of conference 24-28 Aug 2009, Date added to the IEEE Xplore: 6th April 2015.

57. Majumder, A.; Behera, L.; Subramanian(2014), V.K.; "Local binary pattern based facial expression recognition using Self-organizing Map,International Joint Conference on Neural Networks (IJCNN), volume 2 issue 1, July.

58. Manisha, Dr JagjitSingh(2015), Facial Expression Recognition Using Neural Network (IJCSIT) International Journal of Computer Science and Information Technologies, Vol. 6 (3) , pp 3249-3251, June

59. Michel P. and El KalioubyR.(2003), "Real time facial expression recognition in video using support vector machines," in Proceedings of the 5th ACM International conference on Multimodal interfaces(ICMI'03), pp 258–2645th-7th November.

60. Meharabian A. (1968), "Communication without Words" Psychology Today, Vol.2,no.4, pp 53-56.

61. (2016) Measuring Emotions in the Face, Chapter 6, Emotion Measurement, DOI: http://dx.doi.org/10.1016/B978-0-08-100508-8.0000-0, Elsevier.

62. Mehdi AkhariOskuyee (2012), Using Feed Forward Network to Increase the Accuracy in Face Emotion Recognition, International Journal of Advanced Research in Computer Science ,Volume 3, No. 1, Jan-Feb.

63. Michael Balconi, Alberto Granato, FalitYovel, Simon Vamplew, Michela Balconi-Alba Carrea, Michael Houlihan-Lan Fraser, Walter Mahler and Sandra(2007), Emotional face Expressions in Post-traumatic stress disorder, Department of Psychology,Neuropshycological Trends-1/2007.

64. Michel Owayjan, Roger Achkar, Moussa Iskandar (2016), Face Detection with Expression Recognition Using Artificial Neural Networks,2016 3[rd]IEEE-Middle East Conference on Biomedical Engineering(MECOBE), Beirut, pp 115-119, 17 Nov 2016.

65. Mohamed Abubakkarsiddique,M, Selva Ganaesh.B, Ganeshan.R (2014), "ANFIS classifier Based lung Tumor Severity Diagnosis", International journal of Advanced Research in computer science and technology, Vol.3, Issue special1, Jan—Mar.

66. Murthy G.R.S, Jadon R.S(2009), "Effectiveness of Eigenspaces for facial expression recogntion", International Journal of Computer Theory And Engineering, Vol.1 No. 5, 1793-8201,Pp 638-642, December

67. Muhammad Hameed, Siddiqil, Adil,MehmoodKhan,Tae Choong Chung, and Sungyoung Lee (2013),A Precise Recognition Model for Human Facial Expression Recognition System, 26th IEEE Canadian Conference on Electrical and Computer Engineering (CCECE'13),May 2013.

68. Mythiasaithambi, sujatha C, Manoharan and srinivasansubramaniyan (2012), Classification of respiratory abnormalities using ANFIS,Asian Conference on Intelligent Information and Database systems, ACIIDS 2012, Lecture notes in Computer Science Vol 7198, pp 65-73,2012, Springer, Verlag Berlin Heidelberg.

69. NazimaKauser, Jitendra Sharma, "Automatic Facial Expression Recognition: A survey Based on Feature Extraction and Classification Techniques", 2016 International conference on ICT in Business Industry and Governmebt(ICTBIG), Indore, 2016, pp.1-4, date of conference 18-19 Nov 2016, date added to IEEE Xplore 6th April 2017.

70. NazilPerveen,Shubhrata Gupta, Kesari Verma (2012), Facial Expression Recognition System using Statistical Feature and Neural Network, International Journal of Computer Applications (0975 – 888) Volume 48– No.18, June.

71. Neeta Sarode, Shalini Bhatia (2010), Facial Expression recognition, International Journal on Computer Science and Engineering,(IJCSE) Vol. 02, No. 05,pp 1552-1557,February.

72. Neha Gupta, Navneet Kaur (2013),"Design and Implementation of Emotion recognition System by Matlab", International Journal of Engineering Research and Applications(IJERA), Vol. 3, Issue 4, pp. 2002-2006, Jul-Aug.

73. Neha Bhardwaj, Manish Dixit (2016), "A Review: Facial Expression with its Techniques and Application", International Journal of Signal Procession, Image Procession and pattern Recognition, Vol.9, No.6 pp. 149-158, September

74. Nidhi R. Brahmbhatt, Harshadkumar B. Prajapati, Vipul K. Dabhi (2017), "Survey and Analysis of Extraction of

Human Face Features", 2017 Innovations in Poer and Advanced Computing Technologies (i-PACT), Vellore. 2017, pp 1-8, date of Conference 21-22 April 2017, Date Added to IEEE Xplore 04-Jan-2018.

75. Nisha & Sandeep Dahiya (2015), Face Detection and Expression Recognition using Neural Network Approaches, Global Journal of Computer Science and Technology: Volume 15 Issue 3 Version 1.0, year 2015,

76. Paul E Griffiths, Elena Walsh (2015), "Emotion and Expression", International Encyclopedia of the Social and Behavioral Sciences, 2nd edition, Elsevier, Volume 7.

77. Pawel Tarnowski, Marcin Kolodziej, Andrzej Majowski, Remigiusz J. Rak(2017), "Emotion Recognition Using Facial Expressions",Proceedings of International Conference on Computational Sciences(ICCS), paper ID 108, 12-14 June.

78. Premanand P Ghadekar, Hanan Ali Alrikabi, Nilanth B Chopade (2016), "Efficient Face and Facial Expresslion recognition Model", IEEE 2nd international conference on computing communition (ICCUBEA), control and automation 12-13 Aug 2016

79. Prashant P Thakare, Pravin S Patil (2016), Facial Expression Recognition Algorithm Based on KNN Classifier, IJCSn International Journal of Computer Science and Network, Volume 5 Issue 6, December.

80. Rahul s. Agarwal, Urvashi N. Agrawal (2013), "A review of emotion recognition using hybrid classifier", International Journal of Application or Innovation in Engineering and Management, Special Issue for National Conference on Recent advances in technology and Management for integrated growth 2013. (RATMIG-2013).

81. Ryan J. Heeringa(2017), Trauma, PTSD, and the developing Brain, 19 August,

Springer.

1. Ryan Liberty, Mental Health Gifts Book

2. Somayeh., A Machine Learning based Approach for Identifing Traumatic Brain Injury Patients for whom a head CT scan can be avoided, 2016 38th Annual International conference of the IEEE Engineering in Medicine and Biology Society(EMBC),Orlando, PP. 2285-2261,Date of Conference 16-20 Aug 2016, Date Added to IEEE Xplore 18th October 2016.

3. Satyananda Reddy, T. Srinivas (2016), "Improving the classification Accuracy of Emotion Recognition using Facial Expressions", International Journal of Applied Engineering Research, Volume 11, Issue Number 1, pp 650-655,November.

4. Sanjay Kumar , Facial Expression Recognition: A Review, Special Conference Issue: National Conference on Cloud Computing & Big Data, pp. 159-162.

5. Sanaarjit Kar, Sujit Das, PijushKantiGhosh(2014) , Applications of Neuro fuzzy systems. A brief review and future outline, Applied Soft computing, Elesiver, Volume 15, February 2014, Pages 243-259.

6. Sang-Kwon Sim, Jongno-gu, Jun-dong Cho, Jongno-gu (2016), Expression Recognition Based on Artificial Neural Network Using Error Backpropagation Learning Algorithm, International Journal of Applied Engineering Research Volume 11, Number 2 pp 820-823, November.

7. Samiksha Agrawal, Pallavi Khatri, Shashikant Gupta (2015),"Facial Expression Recognition Techniques: A survey", International Journal of Advances in Electronics and Computer Science, Volume-2, Issue-1, Jan.

8. Shamla Mantri, Kalpana Bapat (2011), Neural Network Based Face Recognition Using Matlab, IJCSET, Vol 1, Issue 1,pp 6-9, Feb.

9. ShubhangiGiripunjje, Narendra Bawane, "ANFIS based emotions recognition in speech", International Conference on Knowledge-Based and Intelligent Information and Engineering Systems (KES 2007), Lecture Notes in Compputer Science, Vol. 4692, pp 77-84, Springer, Berlin, Heidelberg.

10. Shruti Bansal and Pravin Nagar (2015), Emotion Recognition from Facial Expression based on Bezier curve, International Journal of Advanced Information Technology(IJAIT) Vol. 5, No. 3/4/5/6, December.

11. Shinde A.R And Agnihotri P.P (2014), "Comparative study of facial feature extraction, expression and emotion recognition", IBMRD's Journal of Management and research, Print ISSN—2277-730. Online ISSN 234-5922, Vol.3, Issue 2, Sep.

12. Shubhada Deshmukh, Manassi Patwardhan, Anjali Mahajan(2015),"Survey on real time facial expression

Recognition techniques" IET Biometrics, Volume 5, Issue 3, September 2016, pp 155-163.

13. Singh S. K., Chauhan D., Vatsa M., and Singh R.(2003), A robust skin color based face detection algorithm, Journal of Science and Engineering, vol. 6, no. 4,pp. 227–234, June.

14. Simon Haykin, *Neural Networks a comprehensive foundation*, Prentice hall 1999.

15. Smriti Tikoo, Nitin Malik (2016), Detection of Face using Viola Jones and Recognition using Back Propagation Neural Network, International Journal of Computer Science and Mobile Computing, Vol.5 Issue.5, pg. 288-295, May.

16. Sonali V.Hedaoo, M.D.Katkar, S.P.Khandait (2014), Feature Tracking and Expression Recognition of Face Using Dynamic Bayesian Network International Journal of Engineering Trends and Technology (IJETT) – Volume 8 Number 10- Feb

17. Somayeh Molael, Frederic K. Korley, SM Reza Soroushmehr, Hayley Falk, HarisSair, Kevin Ward (2016), A Machine Learning based Approach for identifying Traumatic Brain Injury patients for whom a Head CT scan can be Avoided, 2016 38th Annual International conference of the IEEE Engineering in Medicine and Biology Society (EMBC), Orlando, 2016, pp. 2258-2261, date of Conference 16-20 Aug 2016, date Added to IEEE Xplore 18th October 2016.

18. Sunil Kumar, M.K. Bhuyan, Biplab Ketan Chakraborty (2016), "Extraction of informative regions of a face for facial expression recognition", IET Computer Vision, Vol. 10, Issue 6, pp. 567-576, September 2016.

19. Swathi Mishra, Avinash Dhole (2015) ,"AnEffectal approach for facial expression recognition using ANFIS",International Journal of Advanced research in computer and communication engineering vl.44, Issue 5, May.

20. Swathi Mishra, Avinash Dhole (2016)," Design and implementation of Facial expression recognition using adaptive Neuro fuzzy classifier", International Journal of Engineering and Computer Science, Vol.5, Issue 8, page. No. 17555-17561, August.

21. Syed Khaleel Ahmed, Jawad Nagi, FarrukhNagi (2008), A MATLAB based Face Recognition System using Image Processing and Neural Networks, Proceedings on 4th International Colloquium on Signal Processing and its Applications,7th -9th March.

22. Takeo Fujiwara(2015)., "Asssociation between facial expression and PTSD symptoms among young children exposed to the great east Japan earthquake: a pilot study", Frontiers in psychology, Volume 6, Article 1534, October.

23. Tan X and Triggs B(2010), "Enhanced local texture feature sets for face recognition under difficult lighting conditions," Image Processing, IEEE Transactions on, vol. 19, no. 6,pp. 1635–1650, April.

24. Tai S.C., and Chung K.C(2008), "Automatic Facial Expression Recognition System Using Neural Network", TENCON-2007-2007 IEEE Region 10 Conference, Taipei, pp. 1-4,date of conference 30 Oct-2 Nov 2007, date added to IEEE Xplore 14 Jan 2008.

25. Tuhin Kundu, Chandran Saravanan (2017), "Advancements and recent trends in Emotion Recognition using Facial Image Analysis and Machine learning models", 2017 IEEE International Conference on Electrical, Electronics, Communication, Computer and Optimization techniques(ICEECCOT), Mysuru pp. 1-6,Date of conference 15-16 Dec 2017, date added to the IEEE Xplore 8th Feb 2018.

26. Twisha Patel, Bhumia Shah (2017), A Survey on Facial Feature Extraction Techniques for Automatic face Annotation, 2017 IEEE International Conference on Innovative Mechanisms for Industry Application (ICIMIA 2017), pp. 224-228, Date of conference 21-23 Feb 2017, date added to the IEEE Xplore 13 July 2017.

27. Varanya P V, Anu George (2017), Automatic Recognition of Facial Expression Using Features of Salient Patches with SVM and ANN Classifier, Proceeding of International Conference on Trends in Electronics and Informatics(ICEI), August.

28. Viola P., Jones M. J (2004), "Robust real-time face detection," International journal of computer vision, vol. 57, no. 2, pp. 137–154, April.

29. XiaoningChen;Wushan Cheng (2015),Human Facial Expression Recognition Based on Eigen face approach ,International Journal of Computer Science and Engineering Survey(IJCSES), Volume 5,April.

30. Yang., Requirement and Design Analysis for the Post-Trauma Mobile Psychology Service, 2009 IITA International Conference on Services Science, Management and Engineering, Zhangjiajie, pp. 270-273, Date of conference 11-12

July 2009, date added to the IEEE Xplore 4th Sep 2009.

31. Yeshudas Muttu, H.G. Virani (2015), "Effective Face Detection, Feature Extraction and Neural Network based Approaches for Facial Expression recognition", International Conference on Information Processing (ICIP), 16-19 Dec.

32. Yi, Ji, Khalid Idrissi(2010), "Learning from Essential Facial Parts and Local Features for Automatic Facial Expression Recognition,2010 International Workshop on content Based Multimedia Indexing(CBMI), Grenoble, pp. 1-6,Date of conference 23-25 June 2010, date added to the IEEE Xplore 29th July 2010.

33. Zhen Zhou, Yang ji, Chunhong Zhang, Zhouhong Zhu, Wenzhong Wang, Hao wang, Implematation of Post-Trauma Mobile Psychology service Based on MSNS platform ,2010 International conference on Service Sciences, Hangzhou, pp. 309-313,date of conference: 13-14 May 2010, date added to the IEEE Xplore 24 th June 2010.

34. Zhengyou Zhang (2006), Facial expression Classification using Gabor and Log Gabor Filters, Proceedings of the 7th International Conference on Automatic Face and Gesture Recogntion(FGR'06) IEEE computer society, 10th -12th April.

35. L. Zhong, Q. Yang Q, P. Hung, and D.N. Metaxas (2015), "Learning Multiscale Active Facial Patches for Expression Analysis," *IEEE Transcations on Cybernetics*, Vol 45 No.8, pp. 1499-1510, September

36. Zia Uddin, J.J. Lee, and Y.S Kim (2009), "An enhanced independent Component-based human facial expression recognition from video", IEEE Transsactions on Consumer Electronics, Vol 55, No.4, pp.2216-2224, November.